UNDISCOVERED
MUSEUMS OF
NEW YORK

UNDISCOVERED Museums of New York

Eloise Danto

SURREY BOOKS
230 East Ohio Street
Suite 120
Chicago, Illinois 60611

UNDISCOVERED MUSEUMS OF NEW YORK is published by Surrey Books, 230 E. Ohio St., Suite 120, Chicago, Illinois 60611. Phone: (312) 751-7330.

This book is manufactured in the United States of America.

Second edition. 1 2 3 4 5

Library of Congress Cataloging-in-Publication Data

Danto, Eloise.
    Undiscovered museums of New York / by Eloise Danto. — 2nd ed.
      p.   cm.
    Rev. ed. of: Museums of New York. c1989.
    Includes index.
    ISBN 0-940625-36-9 : $8.95
    1. Museums—New York (N.Y.)—Guide-books. 2. New York
(N.Y.)—Description—1981- —Guide-books. I. Danto, Eloise.
Museums of New York. II. Title.
AM13.N5D37 1991   90-24479
069'.09747'1—dc20   CIP

Illustrations and maps by Eloise Danto.

Editorial Production: Bookcrafters, Inc., Chicago.
Cover Design: Hughes & Co., Chicago.
Typesetting: On Track Graphics, Inc., Chicago.

Single copies of this book may be ordered by sending check or money order for $10.95 (includes postage and handling) per book to Surrey Books at the above address.

The "Undiscovered Museums" series is distributed to the trade by Publishers Group West.

Cover Photos *(clockwise from top):*

Studio Museum in Harlem is becoming a world center of black art.

Liberty's original "torch and flame," on exhibit in the Statue's base.

American Craft Museum exhibits in their dramatic stairwell.

The Cloisters, a quiet retreat.

All photos courtesy New York Convention & Visitors Bureau.

Other Books in This Series:

Undiscovered Museums of London
Undiscovered Museums of Paris
Undiscovered Museums of Florence

**To Mark, Rachel, Hannah,
Eryn, Ben and Colleen**

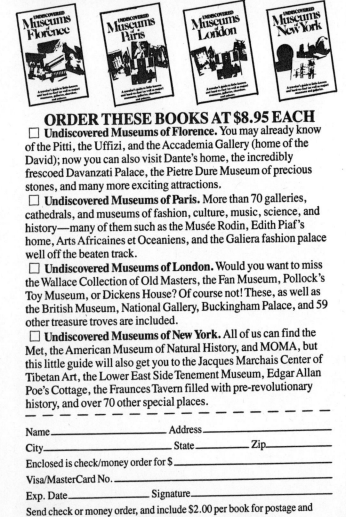

ACKNOWLEDGMENTS

One of the happiest aspects of writing this book was the contribution of time, energy, and devotion on the part of various people whoe donated their individual energies to its completion. To Bettina Seifert-Guerakhan, who conducted diligent research forays across Staten Island into and through its museums; to Harold Goldfarb and Stanley Disenhof, who trekked across Queens and into its museums; to Randy and Benjamin Danto, who chauffeured me across the bridges, through the tunnels, along the highways, and around the neighborhoods of New York's five boroughs; to Jayne Rattiner, who looked after me during my months of painstaking research and contributed insights and New York smarts toward the completion of my mission; to Colleen Niesen, who came through for me at the midnight hour; and to my friends and family who stood patiently in the wings while the work came to fruition, I acknowledge my everlasting, heartfelt thanks. Last, but not least, my thanks to you, the reader, that very special traveler, without whom this guidebook series would never have come to pass.

E.D.

TABLE OF CONTENTS
(by Borough)

INTRODUCTION

In addition to the many giant megamuseums in New York, this book also contains almost all of its smaller, middle-size, and "undiscovered" museums, that is, the hardly-known-about museums, the museums that may never reach the pages of large, cumbersome guidebooks. These attractions may never be mentioned in the lengthy coverage of popular tourist meccas. Many residents of New York itself have never even discovered the existence of these museums, some of which have only one room; some contain private collections. In almost all instances, once the traveler is introduced to the new museum, he or she suddenly gains insight and an intimate pleasure in that discovery, drawing closer to the history, dynamics, culture, and personality of the city.

New York is one of the world's greatest art centers, the ultimate mecca for art collectors, art dealers, and, naturally, the artists who create art. New York has been accused of being glitzy, glamorous, awesome, flamboyant, intimidating, angry, and a profusion of other things, both complimentary and uncomplimentary. There is no denying that it possesses all of these characteristics and more. New York is also one of the most exciting and complicated cities in the Western World and cannot be fully appreciated without realizing that fact through the incredible number and diversity of its museums. Every mode of expression is found in one or another of New York's museums, unequalled in scope, quality, and number of treasures. Its five boroughs contain some of the most definitive collections of esoteric, experimental, alternative, avant-garde, and conventional art found anywhere.

This astonishing city is at the center of the crossroads of many cultures. Its museums represent dozens of countries and hundreds of traditions. These treasure houses range from simple or primitive arts within a one-room museum to slick, sophisticated, self-contained complexes, spread out across several city blocks. Some are one of a kind in the world; others might be two or three of one kind.

New York is host to 17 million out-of-towners annually. Of this number, roughly 65 percent are museum-goers to one degree or another. Another exciting aspect to the diversity of New York's museums is the opportunity of visiting the city's varied neighborhoods, from the elite Museum Mile of Fifth Avenue to the pre-revolutionary Quaker homes in Flushing and Queens to early New Amsterdam locations in lower Manhattan to the patriotic Statue of Liberty/Ellis Island/Castle Clinton triangle, and on to a surprising Staten Island with six fine museums.

Museum-going and interest in art and cultural matters is at an all-time high. The modern world has become more complex, the pace of current lifestyles has speeded up, and as a result, New York museum managements feel even more responsible to their patrons. I discovered, as I visited the museums, that the people who manage them are fiercely dedicated to the preservation and success of their institutions. Their profession often becomes manifest as loving devotion, not unlike a close family community, enhancing each museum's uniqueness.

Another aspect of museum management is the development of mailing lists. Within the past decade New York museums have expended vast sums of money to publish and promote mail order catalogs, not only for the sale of postal cards, books, and posters but also to offer faithful replicas of current exhibition items and permanent inventory. Museums that develop and maintain elaborate direct selling programs fare much better financially than those that do not. In addition, the more highly developed museum shops generate added income.

How does a museum survive? Through membership plans tailored to fit the needs and income of its varied subscribers; through educational programs, film series, concerts, lectures, children's programs, and organized trips; through gift shops that offer a range of gifts from 25-cent postal cards to substantial works of art that cost thousands of dollars; through highly polished public relations departments constantly reaching out to clientele; and through securing the very finest in both permanent and temporary exhibitions.

Not all of New York's museums are found in Manhattan. Brooklyn and Queens each have seven, the Bronx and Staten Island each have six, and Washington Heights has five. The remaining fifty or so are scattered throughout Manhattan, reaching from Battery Park on up to Washington Heights at the northernmost tip of Manhattan Island.

New York has more ethnic/religious museums than any other city in the world—11 to be exact. They include African, Native American, Chinese, Japanese, Jewish, Hispanic, and black. These are in addition to its historic, scientific, social, fine arts, and miscellaneous museums. If you have a particular interest or preference, there's a museum here for you. In fact, there is an attraction for the museum person in all of us.

Nestled among New York's major museums are some lesser-known and smaller ones not to be overlooked. Some of your most intimate, rewarding visits will be made to the smaller museums. Don't rush past any of them; there might be a superb little collection within. Make it a point to visit a number of New York's smaller, undiscovered museums such as the Old Merchants House or the Lower East Side Tenement Museum in Lower Manhattan, and the Edgar Allan Poe Cottage in the Bronx.

The New York art audience has an insatiable taste for good art, and so some of its spectacular events generate crowd crunching. Keep this in mind when attending special exhibitions; invariably, it's going to be equally good and crowded.

The writer gives warning to the overly enthusiastic museum-goer. Be wary of that familiar state of panic, the symptom of too much art and too much learning in too brief a time. Plan your day carefully, keeping to a certain area of the city. To avoid criss-crossing, study your local map before starting out and decide on an orderly plan of attack. You should have a street map of all five boroughs, a subway map, and an excellent map called "Artwise Manhattan," all three available at book stores. Keep these with you and don't hesitate to use them. You'll save infinite time and frustration. Maintain a steady pace, and do not, under any circumstances, plan on doing a museum marathon, for that is a guaranteed disaster.

When planning your day's museum journey, get into the habit of telephoning to verify the days and hours of opening. Remember, 95 percent of New York's museums are closed on Monday. A few are open only one or two days a week. The majority of Museum Mile museums offer free entry Tuesday evenings. Most of the larger museums have fixed entry fees; others will request a suggested contribution. If you are a senior citizen, ID should be presented for a discount. Children are often admitted free. All of this information is covered in each museum's section, and it is also posted at all museum entrances .

If you are traveling with children, New York offers several special-for-kids museums. I've included these in one section called "Kids' Museums" at the back of the book.

My system of star ratings is based on the quality of each museum's contents, its manner of presentation, lighting, dating of displayed art, explanations, the sense of order, and the degree of professionalism. One star represents the least value and four stars the highest.

There are two indexes at the back of the book: "Index by Types of Museums" and "General Index."

The writer fervently hopes that the information presented in this simplified volume will assist you, the art and museum traveler, in your search for exciting and interesting cultural experiences. Even though I have barely introduced New York's eighty museums, if I have enhanced your awareness of them only slightly, it will not have been time lost. Join me now in an unusual adventure of exploration and discovery, down the streets of a fabulous city and into the galleries, museums, major and minor cultural attractions of New York.

THE MUSEUMS OF NEW YORK

LOWER MANHATTAN

LOWER MANHATTAN

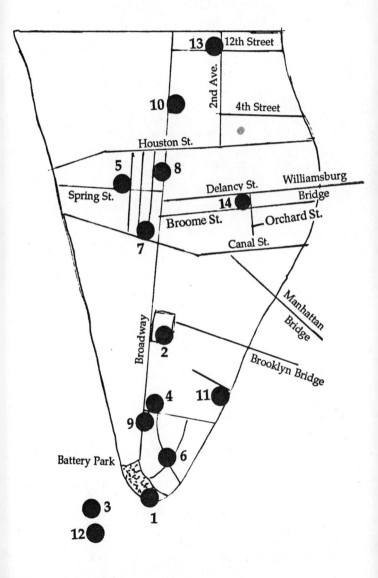

CASTLE CLINTON NATIONAL MONUMENT

OPEN:	*Daily year round: Summer 8-8:30; Winter 9-5*	ENTRY:	*Free*
		TYPE:	*Historical*
		ADDRESS:	*Battery Park*
		TEL:	*212-344-7220*
CLOSED:	*Christmas, New Year's Day*	GIFT SHOP:	*No*
		CAFE:	*No*
SUB:	*IRT #4,5 to Bowling Green*	KIDS:	*No*
		RATING:	★★
BUS:	*M6, M15 to South Ferry*		

Here is one of New York's small museums. It's just one room, semicircular in shape, conforming to the contour of the former fort in which it's contained. You can't miss it: It's right in the middle of Battery Park.

During the past 180 years the monument has enjoyed the tenancy of the military as a fort (1812), actors as an entertainment center (1824), immigrants as an immigration center until the establishment of Ellis Island (1855), and fish as the New York Aquarium (1930s). Drawings, lithographs, and exhibits line the walls, giving a chronological history of the monument from 1812 to the present.

Castle Clinton, together with the Statue of Liberty and Ellis Island, form a three-pronged historical museum complex. Just walk across the courtyard to buy your tickets for the ferry to the museum within the Statue and/ or newly refurbished Ellis Island.

CITY HALL GOVERNORS ROOM

OPEN:	*Mon.-Fri. 10-4*	ENTRY:	*Free*
CLOSED:	*Sat., Sun., &*	TYPE:	*Historical*
	Holidays	ADDRESS:	*City Hall Park*
SUB:	*N,R, to City Hall*	TEL:	*212-566-5525*
	IRT #4,5,6 to	GIFT SHOP:	*No*
	Brooklyn Bridge	CAFE:	*No*
BUS:	*M1, M6 to City*	KIDS:	*Yes*
	Hall	RATING:	★★★

The City Hall building, fronted by one of New York's tiniest parks and not 50 feet away from the Brooklyn Bridge, is small and stately. It's worth coming here just to see this little gem. Once inside, walk toward the rotunda, climb the circular marble stairway, and you are there.

The museum is composed of one central room and two conference chambers. Presidential portraits by the renowned John Trumbull line the walls, along with plenty of historic memorabilia. There's Washington's writing table and some gorgeous period furnishings.

This museum visit is clean, quick, and austere with a touch of dignity. After all, the mayor of New York presides in the next chamber. Then there are the quarters of the Executive Branch and the City Council of New York, all ceremoniously guarded.

ELLIS ISLAND

OPEN:	*Year round, 10-4*	**ENTRY:**	*Free*
CLOSED:	*Christmas, New Year's Day*	**TYPE:**	*Historical*
		ADDRESS:	*Ellis Island*
FERRY:	*Year round, daily 10-4, every hour from Battery Park*	**TEL:**	*212-363-3200*
		GIFT SHOP:	*Yes*
		CAFE:	*Yes*
		KIDS:	*Yes*
		RATING:	*★★★★*

In 1890, construction was begun on Ellis Island as a receiving and processing immigration center in New York Harbor. Between 1892 and 1954, a mere 62 years, almost 17 million people entered through it into the United States. It was the largest human migration in modern history. Ellis Island is one mile off the lower tip of Manhattan.

Over the years the complex and its facilities deteriorated, and in 1964 work was begun to restore the waiting rooms, dormitories , hospital, telegraph station, train ticketing office, kitchens, dining rooms, and, of course, the imposing Great Room, where the official museum is now located. This has been the most expensive refurbishment in the nation's history. The Beaux-Arts main building is now transformed into a majestic monument to those masses of immigrants, and the original atmosphere of anxious drama is projected through photographs and films.

One can trace one's ancestry by means of computers at the Family History Center. For a $100 donation, your ancestors' names will be engraved on the copper-paneled, waist-high wall that surrounds the museum. Welcome back, Ellis Island.

Get on a shuttle boat to the Statue of Liberty, the sister landmark to Ellis. Ferries run every half-hour. I guarantee you a thrilling day in New York Harbor.

FEDERAL HALL NATIONAL MONUMENT

OPEN:	*Mon.-Fri. 9-5*	ENTRY:	*Free*
CLOSED:	*Sat., Sun., &*	TYPE:	*Historical*
	Holidays except	ADDRESS:	*26 Wall St. at*
	Washington's		*Nassau St.*
	Birthday and	TEL:	*212-264-8711*
	July 4	GIFT SHOP:	*No*
SUB:	*IRT #2,3,4 to*	CAFE:	*No*
	Wall St.	KIDS:	*Yes*
BUS:	*M1, M6, M15 to*	RATING:	★★★
	South Ferry		

The building was constructed in 1699 and is one of New York's oldest. Originally it was the City Hall, then the Customs House, and thereafter constantly used as one federal agency or another. It enjoys distinction as the site of George Washington's inauguration in 1789.

The museum upstairs holds cabinets and cases filled with Washingtonia as well as all sorts of information about the Republic, the Revolutionary War, and the Constitution. In the early years of our nation, New York City was the nation's capital, and it was beset with the not unusual urban problems of water pollution, the need for parks, and a shortage of funds. George Washington dominates the entire atmosphere; he presides outside the building in stately bronze.

FIREFIGHTING MUSEUM

OPEN:	*Tues.-Sat. 10-4*	TYPE:	*Miscellaneous*
CLOSED:	*Sun., Mon. &*	ADDRESS:	*278 Spring St.*
	Holidays	TEL:	*212-691-1303*
SUB:	*IND C,E,K to*	GIFT SHOP:	*Yes*
	Spring St.	CAFE:	*No*
BUS:	*M6,M8,M10 to*	KIDS:	*Yes*
	Spring St.	RATING:	★★★
ENTRY:	*Adult $3;*		
	Child $1		

Does your pulse race when you hear the roar of a fire engine? Ever wonder why the Dalmatian is the mascot of fire houses? Well, don't miss this museum. It's a former fire house, three stories high, with bright red doors.

The collection on the main floor presents firefighting memorabilia. It traces the history of firefighting through vehicles, equipment, and fire trucks. The second floor captures the tradition and pageantry of early firefighting and presents an exhibit of some of New York's spectacular fires and fire engines. There's a library containing records and files, photographs of engines, and portraits of fire officials.

FRAUNCES TAVERN

OPEN:	*Mon.-Fri. 10-4; Sun. 12-4*	**TYPE:**	*Historical*
CLOSED:	*Saturday & Holidays*	**ADDRESS:**	*54 Pearl St. at B'way.*
SUB:	*IND R, N to Whitehall St.*	**TEL:**	*212-425-1776*
		GIFT SHOP:	*Yes*
BUS:	*M1, M6 to South Ferry*	**CAFE:**	*Yes*
		KIDS:	*Yes*
ENTRY:	*Adult $2.50; Sr. & Student $1*	**RATING:**	★★★

There really was a Sam Fraunces. He was the West Indian steward of George Washington who bought this building and turned it into a tavern, which became a popular gathering place for prominent citizens of early New York. At the turn of the 20th century, the tavern was restored and preserved as a museum. It's one flight up and is composed of three rooms that focus on the history and culture of New York at the time of the Revolutionary War, plus the room where George Washington bid his historic farewell to his officers.

Documents, drawings, and lithographs line the walls, and period furnishings are placed about. The museum is beautifully maintained in meticulous detail, appearing as it did 200 years ago. Workshops, concerts, and theatrical performances are hosted here. There's a tiny gift shop, and the small restaurant downstairs has an excellent menu for either lunch or dinner.

MUSEUM OF HOLOGRAPHY

OPEN:	*Daily 11-6; Wed. til 8*	ADDRESS:	*11 Mercer St.*
		TEL:	*212-925-0526*
SUB:	*Lex #6 to Canal St.*	GIFT SHOP:	*Yes*
ENTRY:	*Adult $3.50; Sr. & Student $2.50*	CAFE:	*No*
		KIDS:	*Yes*
TYPE:	*Miscellaneous*	RATING:	*★*

Holography is a uniquely creative art form invented here in the 1940s, and it is neither widely understood nor fully appreciated. Simply put, it's the exposure of photographic film to a laser beam that creates a three-dimensional image. The effect is somewhat eerie, for the image transforms as the viewer moves about in front of it, thus changing the visual effect by distance and angle.

The main floor of this museum has an assortment of holograms varying in size from a few inches to several feet. Downstairs there is a permanent exhibit and a small theater for video films on holography. Unfortunately, the museum, despite the appeal of its subject, is dusty and shabby, and it needs either refurbishing, a facelift, or both. The good news is your stroll along Canal Street for some of New York's raved-about shopping bargains.

NEW MUSEUM OF CONTEMPORARY ART

OPEN:	*Wed., Thurs., Sun. 12-6; Fri., Sat. 12-8*	**TYPE:**	*Fine Arts*
		ADDRESS:	*583 B'way. at Spring St.*
CLOSED:	*Mon., Tues., & Holidays*	**TEL:**	*212-219-1222*
SUB:	*IRT #6 to Spring St.*	**GIFT SHOP:**	*Yes*
BUS:	*5th Ave. #1 to B'way. & Houston*	**CAFE:**	*No*
		KIDS:	*Yes*
ENTRY:	*Adult $2.50 Sr. & Student $1.50*	**RATING:**	★★★

This museum, open since 1983, is relatively unknown and may not be listed in all guidebooks. It's located in the Soho district, which, when translated, means South of Houston (Street). Innovative, contemporary collections of living artists are shown on a rotating basis.

Major exhibitions originating here represent imaginative, offbeat, and eclectic art, all exciting. The museum publishes its own art-related books. Their library, called the Soho Center Library for Contemporary Art, is open to critics, scholars, art professionals, and art aficionados. This is a serious, intelligent museum; small but good, with sparkling presence. I recommend it.

NEW YORK STOCK EXCHANGE

OPEN:	Mon.-Fri. 10-4	**ADDRESS:**	20 Broad St. at
CLOSED:	Sat., Sun., &		Wall St.
	Holidays	**TEL:**	212-656-5167
SUB:	7th Ave. #2,3	**GIFT SHOP:**	Yes
	to Wall St.	**CAFE:**	No
ENTRY:	Free	**KIDS:**	No
TYPE:	Miscellaneous	**RATING:**	★★★

How many times have you been to New York and never entertained the notion of visiting the Stock Exchange? Well, get in line for the 10 a.m. opening, take the elevator upstairs, and move through several rooms to the glass-enclosed balcony overlooking the trading floor. It's pure pandemonium and difficult to believe that those scurrying figures below know what they're doing.

You'll learn quite a bit about trading, international financial matters, and the system of those red electronic numbers flashing across the walls. A six-minute film explains the fundamentals and mechanics of the Market. You can buy a NYSE tee-shirt at the gift shop. Please call first—this attraction is temporarily closed for restoration.

OLD MERCHANTS HOUSE

OPEN:	*Sunday 1-4; Commercial tours only on weekdays*	**ENTRY:**	*Adult $3; Sr. & Student $2*
		TYPE:	*Historical*
CLOSED:	*month of August*	**ADDRESS:**	*29 E. 4 St.*
		TEL:	*212-777-1089*
SUB:	*IND A,B,D,E,F to 4th St. IRT Lex #6 to Astor Pl.*	**GIFT SHOP:**	*Yes*
		CAFE:	*No*
		KIDS:	*No*
		RATING:	★★★

The Old Merchants House is a rare treasure built in 1832 by Joseph Brewster and bought two years later by the Treadwell family, who were maritime and houseware and hardware merchants. With the exception of the draperies and carpeting, all furnishings are original and still glistening. The house truly reflects the fashionable lifestyle of a typical upper-middleclass New York family. Subsequent Treadwell generations remained here until 1933, when the last of the family died.

The house is laden with heavy Victoriana—from Greek Revival parlors to Gothic Revival bed chambers—and if you peek into the closets, you'll find handsome period clothing and accessories. Intimate family memorabilia are sprinkled about. The kitchen was apparently the center of family activities, with its cast iron stove, brick oven, and sink with a hand pump. There's an aura of privacy throughout the entire house, almost as though someone from this family might suddenly appear, offended by our intrusion. Restoration is currently going on, and Old Merchants House will reopen in October, 1991.

SOUTH STREET SEAPORT MUSEUM

OPEN:	*10-5 daily*	ADDRESS:	*John St. at East River*
SUB:	*IRT #2,3 to Fulton St.; IRT Lex #4,5 Fulton St.*	TEL:	*212-669-9424*
		GIFT SHOP:	*Yes*
BUS:	*2nd Ave. to Fulton St.*	CAFE:	*No*
		KIDS:	*Yes*
ENTRY:	*Adult $5; Sr. & Student $3*	RATING:	★★
TYPE:	*Miscellaneous*		

There really is a museum, just look for it on John Street at the River. It has ship models, maritime paintings, and memorabilia of ocean liners. But it's the seaport complex that draws the crowds. It's spread out across a half-mile under Brooklyn Bridge, with trendy shops and eateries; and at the river's edge there are several tall ships, boardable and sailable for a New York Harbor cruise.

Be prepared for crowds with high energy levels and stores with prices to match. In 1820 Robert Fulton started a ferry service from here to Brooklyn, put his name on a street and a fish market, and the rest is history. If you can get past the din, South Street Seaport is a fun try at remembering an historic district of Old New York.

STATUE OF LIBERTY

OPEN:	*Daily 10-4*	TYPE:	*Historical*
CLOSED:	*Christmas, New Year's Day*	ADDRESS:	*Liberty Island*
		TEL:	*212-363-3267*
FERRY:	*From Battery Park, daily every half-hour, 9-4; tickets shared with Ellis Island: Adult $6; Sr. & Student $3*	GIFT SHOP:	*Yes*
		CAFE:	*No*
		KIDS:	*Yes*
		RATING:	★★★★

Along with the Mona Lisa in Paris, Liberty is surely one of the most celebrated women in the world, a stirring sight majestically rising out of New York Harbor. Thanks to French sculptor F. A. Bartholdi and Gustave Eiffel, designer of the Eiffel Tower in Paris, plus hundreds of craftsmen and thousands of contributors from many nations, Liberty is the symbol of friendship, freedom, compassion, and courage. In 1986, for her 100th birthday, her radiant luster was gloriously restored.

The Museum within the Statue thrillingly recounts the history of her creation, through drawings, photos, and models, from the original concept to permanent positioning in New York Harbor. Since Liberty is one of New York's most popular attractions, be prepared for long lines unless you arrive early. If you're up to it, a climb of 22 stories will bring you to Liberty's crown for a panoramic view of New York Harbor. By the way, there is a duplicate, smaller version of Liberty that stands in the Seine River in Paris, close to the Pte. de Grenelle (16th arrondissement).

UKRAINIAN MUSEUM

OPEN:	*Wed.-Sun. 1-5*	TYPE:	*Ethnic*
CLOSED:	*Mon., Tues., major Holidays*	ADDRESS:	*203 2nd Ave. at 12 St.*
SUB:	*IRT Lex #4,5,6 to 14 St., Union Square*	TEL:	*212-228-0110*
		GIFT SHOP:	*Yes*
		CAFE:	*No*
ENTRY:	*Adult $1; Sr. & Student $.50*	KIDS:	*No*
		RATING:	★★★

This museum, brimming with ethnicity, occupies the fourth and fifth floors of a renovated brownstone. Its collections are folk art crafts from the 19th and 20th centuries. Ukrainian history is chronicled through photos, drawings, and costume displays. There's a case of intricately painted eggs. You must have seen them at one time or another and may not have realized their origin. The eggs are traditional folk art symbols of fertility and spring rites. Classes are given for egg painting, embroidery, bead stringing, and making holiday decorations. The museum, an important center for the Ukrainian community, devotes itself to increasing public awareness of this relatively unknown culture.

LOWER EAST SIDE TENEMENT MUSEUM

OPEN:	*Tues.-Fri. 11-4;*	ENTRY:	*Free*
	Sun. 10-3	TYPE:	*Historical*
CLOSED:	*Saturday &*	ADDRESS:	*97 Orchard St.*
	Monday	TEL:	*212-431-0233*
SUB:	*IND F to*	GIFT SHOP:	*No*
	Delancy St.	CAFE:	*No*
BUS:	*M15 to Allen &*	KIDS:	*No*
	Delancy Sts.	RATING:	★★★

The museum is contained within a portion of this six-story building, which was then known as "97 Orchard Street." It's the first living-history museum to honor urban pioneers—blacks, Irish, Germans, Chinese, eastern European Jews, and Italians who arrived in New York during the years between 1865 and 1935 with glowing hopes of a better life. In 1988 work began to memorialize the mood and personality of tenement life that endured in these tiny rooms, once crowded with immigrants who arrived with their paper suitcases and meager belongings.

The phenomena of those times are touchingly brought back to life through photographs, furnishings, and memorabilia.

Programs are presented, films are shown, and a special treat is offered—guided walking tours that highlight the neighborhood's multicultural life and history. A national search is under way to locate former residents, or their descendants, whose roots are at 97 Orchard Street. And so the poignant memory lingers on.

MURRAY HILL

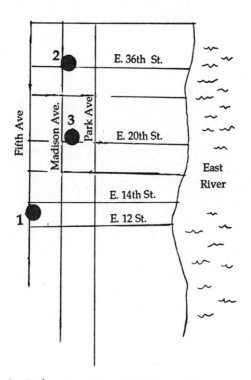

1. Forbes Magazine Galleries, p. 28
2. Pierpont Morgan Library, p. 30
3. Theodore Roosevelt Birthplace, p. 31

FORBES MAGAZINE GALLERIES

OPEN:	Tues., Wed., Fri., Sat 10-4; Thurs: tours by reservation only	BUS:	M1, M2, M3 to 14 St.
		ENTRY:	Free
		TYPE:	General
CLOSED:	Sun., Mon. & Holidays	ADDRESS:	62 5th Ave. at 12 St.
SUB:	IRT #1,2,3,9 to 14 St.; BMT #3,4,5 to 14 St.	TEL:	212-206-5548
		GIFT SHOP:	No
		CAFE:	No
		KIDS:	Yes
		RATING:	★★★★

The Galleries, located on the ground floor of the Forbes Building, feature the holdings of the Forbes Magazine collection. Once inside, your course has been plotted out for you. Begin with Ships Ahoy. Behind eight gold and glass panels from the French flagship, The Normandie, are displayed over 500 antique toy boats. Next is On Parade, a corps of miniature toy armies, featuring soldiers portraying glorious battles of past centuries. Next is the Trophies Gallery, a collection of prizes gathered worldwide from teams, groups, and individuals for various events. Then on to the Manuscript and Autograph

Galleries, with personal letters, documents, and memorabilia of American presidents.

Off the centered lobby is the Fabergé Room, where a dazzling collection of Imperial Easter eggs, *objets d'art*, and jeweled treasures of the Russian czars are displayed. Also off the central lobby is the Picture Gallery, which displays changing exhibitions of European and American paintings and photographs. In less than two hours, you've had an extraordinary museum visit.

PIERPONT MORGAN LIBRARY

OPEN:	Tues.-Sat. 10:30-5; Sun. 1-5	TYPE:	General
CLOSED:	Monday & Holidays	ADDRESS:	29 E. 36 St. at Madison Ave.
SUB:	IND E, F, to 34 St.	TEL:	212-685-0008
		GIFT SHOP:	Yes
BUS:	M1, M2, M3, M4 to 34 St.	CAFE:	No
		KIDS:	Yes
ENTRY:	Donation: Adult $3; Sr. & Student $1	RATING:	★★★★

The library was built for Mr. Morgan at the beginning of this century. Its purpose is twofold. First, it is a center for scholarly research. Second, it is one of New York's most distinguished museums. Mr. Morgan was a rich, crusty, and powerful philanthropist, with consuming interests in music, literature, the arts, history, and an elegant lifestyle. His collections of Old Master drawings, sculptures, illuminated medieval and Renaissance manuscripts, musical manuscripts, early printed books and bindings, and first-edition children's books are among the finest in the world. His study is a museum in itself, with paneled ceilings, rich wood walls, paintings, and massive furnishings. The Library exhibits drawings, autographed manuscripts, and rare books drawn from Mr. Morgan's private collection. This is a virtual treasure house.

THEODORE ROOSEVELT BIRTHPLACE

OPEN:	*Wed.-Sun. 9-5*	TYPE:	*Historical*
CLOSED:	*Mon., Tues. &*	ADDRESS:	*28 E. 20 St.*
	Holidays	TEL:	*212-260-1616*
SUB:	*IRT #6 to 23 St.*	GIFT SHOP:	*Yes*
BUS:	*M1, M2, M3 to*	CAFE:	*No*
	Park Ave. &	KIDS:	*Yes*
	21 St.	RATING:	★★★
ENTRY:	*Adult $1; Sr. &*		
	Student free		

This brownstone witnessed the birth and formative years of T.R., frail, fragile, and asthmatic until, at the age of 12, he commenced rigorous training and developed into a robust, aggressive young man, becoming passionately involved with the American Museum of Natural History. He published essays and books on natural history and public affairs, took expeditions to Africa and South America, created some of our national parks and game preserves, and hunted big game. Roosevelt was a rancher and cowboy, galloping with and heading the Rough

Riders in the Spanish-American War. He was governor of New York, president of the U.S., Nobel Peace Prize winner, and more.

The museum has been restored beautifully to its original dignified grace and Victorian high fashion. Some furnishings are original and all rooms are bursting with Teddy memorabilia. There's even a small teddy bear in a showcase. Here was a home filled with much love and extraordinary family devotion, which still prevails.

MIDTOWN EAST

1. IBM Gallery of Science and Art, p. 34
2. Japan Society, p. 35
3. Museum of Broadcasting, p. 36

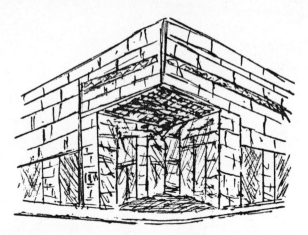

IBM GALLERY OF SCIENCE AND ART

OPEN:	*Tues.-Sat. 11-6*	ADDRESS:	*590 Madison*
CLOSED:	*Sun., Mon. &*		*Ave. at 56 St.*
	Holidays	TEL:	*212-745-6100*
SUB:	*IND E, F to 5th*	GIFT SHOP:	*No*
	Ave.	CAFE:	*No*
ENTRY:	*Free*	KIDS:	*Yes*
TYPE:	*General*	RATING	★★★★

To begin with, IBM has been more than generous in its support of the arts since its founding in the 1930s. The reason I've included the gallery in this museum book is that it ranks as high as some museums for its significant and innovative range of exhibitions in science and the arts. All shows are temporary, each remaining approximately two months. The downstairs auditorium runs continuous art-related films.

Because of the high quality of its exhibitions of folk art, Native American art, Japanese woodblocks, IBM's own collections, scientific exhibitions, and fine art shows, the IBM Gallery rates as an important art center in New York and should be visited. It's also one of the best in manner of presentation, level of professionalism, and quality of exhibitions. And it's all free.

JAPAN SOCIETY

OPEN:	*Mon.-Fri. 9:30-5*	ADDRESS:	*333 E. 47 St. at*
CLOSED:	*Sat. & Sun.*		*1st Ave.*
SUB:	*IRT #6 to 51 St.*	TEL:	*212-752-0824*
BUS:	*M15, M27 to*	GIFT SHOP:	*No*
	47 St.	CAFE:	*No*
ENTRY:	*Free*	KIDS:	*No*
TYPE:	*Ethnic*	RATING:	★★★

This building of authentic modern Japanese design is the only one of its kind in New York. Located directly across from the United Nations, the Society attracts a large Asian following. On entering, you'll see a reflecting pool from which small bamboo trees rise. Maryell Semal, the museum's Assistant Director, sat with me in a cool, high-ceilinged room that looked out into a serene inner courtyard and spoke of the purpose of the Society: It cultivates and enhances the Japan/U.S. relationship in a cultural, artistic, intellectual, and political sense.

Temporary exhibitions, music festivals, films, folk ballets, and tours to Japan are ongoing. Lectures on international business are held for both the American and Japanese communities. Japan Society proves that an intelligent venture can help fuse two cultures.

MUSEUM OF BROADCASTING

OPEN:	*Wed.-Sat. 12-5;*	TYPE:	*Media*
	Tues. 12-8	ADDRESS:	*1East 53 St.*
CLOSED:	*Sun. & Mon.*	TEL:	*212-752-4690*
SUB:	*IRT Lex #4,5,6*	GIFT SHOP:	*Yes*
	to 51 St.	CAFE:	*No*
BUS:	*5th Ave. to 53 St.*	KIDS:	*Yes*
ENTRY:	*Suggested*	RATING:	★★★★
	donation: Adult		
	$4.50; Sr. &		
	Student $3.50		

This brand-new museum is really a mammoth archive of tapes of radio and TV programming and advertisements from 1920 to the present, crammed full of old favorites. Every major public event ever filmed is available for your individual screening. Go up to the fourth-floor library and select your program from the computer-generated catalog. You will be given your own console.

Just to mention a few of the tapes you'll find: Edward R. Morrow's "This Is London," FDR's Fireside Chats, early

Beatles, space shots, moon landings, Sid Caesar, Ernie Kovacs, wartime newsreels, and more. Retrospectives are shown in the main floor theater. The vast microfiche library contains myriad radio scripts. Saturday screenings for kids, too. This museum enjoys great attendance, and why not? What a fun adventure for all! Future plans involve a move to larger quarters on 52nd Street, date unknown.

MIDTOWN WEST

1. American Craft Museum, p. 39
2. Intrepid, p. 40
3. Museum of Modern Art, p. 41
4. New York Public Library, p. 43

AMERICAN CRAFT MUSEUM

OPEN:	*Wed.-Sun. 10-5; Tues. 10-8*	**TYPE:**	*Fine Arts*
CLOSED:	*Monday & Holidays*	**ADDRESS:**	*40 W. 53 St.*
		TEL:	*212-956-6047*
SUB:	*IND E,F to 5th Ave.*	**GIFT SHOP:**	*Yes*
		CAFE:	*No*
BUS:	*M1, M2, M3 to 53 St.*	**KIDS:**	*Yes*
ENTRY:	*Adult $3.50; Sr. & Student $1.50*	**RATING:**	★★★★

The American Craft Council maintains a role of leadership in the U.S. craft movement, and here is the premiere showcase for their craft forms, both traditional and innovative, with accent on the latter. Thanks to the Council, crafts have come to be recognized as a major force in the panoramic placement of art.

An exciting component of this museum is its atrium and central stairway, which give sweeping visibility to four levels of the unique art forms currently appearing. Shows present architecture, furnishings, sculpture, ceramics, glass, fiber, wood and metal, plus many additional media categories, all of particular originality and lovingly displayed.

INTREPID

OPEN:	Wed.-Sun. 10-5	TYPE:	Miscellaneous
CLOSED:	Mon. & Tues.	ADDRESS:	West 46 St. at
SUB:	All lines to 42		Hudson River
	St.; then Cross-	TEL:	212-245-2533
	town Bus M42	GIFT SHOP:	Yes
BUS:	M42 to Carrier	CAFE:	No
ENTRY:	Adult $7; Sr. &	KIDS:	Yes
	Student $6	RATING:	★★★

The heroic carrier Intrepid opened her doors as the Sea-Air-Space Museum in 1981. She is more than impressive; she's downright patriotic. Here is a presentation of naval might and heroism in war with larger-than-life photos, exhibits, and aircraft from Kitty Hawk on up to the Gulf War, including the Patriot and other missiles used there.

What American is not thrilled to see aircraft parked on the Flight Deck, the Combat Information Center, the Hangar Deck, with exhibit halls presenting nothing less than sheer adventure, plus a movie theater with thrilling footage of carrier takeoffs, landings, and flight operations accompanied by great sound effects from radio's war years, 1940s music, and voices of Intrepid's crew during combat situations. If you've ever wondered about the tension on board a carrier, visualize taking off or landing a speeding jet on this runway!

MUSEUM OF MODERN ART

OPEN:	*Fri.-Tues. 11-6; Thurs. 11-9*	TYPE:	*Fine Arts*
CLOSED:	*Wednesday*	ADDRESS:	*11 W. 53 St. at 5th Ave.*
SUB:	*IND E,F to 5th Ave. at 53 St.*	TEL:	*212-708-9480*
BUS:	*M1, M2, M3, M4 to 52 St.*	GIFT SHOP:	*Yes*
		CAFE:	*Yes*
ENTRY:	*Adult $7; Sr. & Student $4*	KIDS:	*Yes*
		RATING:	★★★★

MOMA is at the top of our list, with its white marble and glass facade and unrivalled collection of Modern Art from the 19th century to the present. In addition to its superb painting and sculpture galleries, there are architectural, industrial, and graphic design collections, cinema, furniture and photography collections, drawings and prints—and all are the *crème de la crème*. Artists included in the permanent collection are Rodin, Calder,

Moore, Gaugin, Van Gogh, Pollack, and Redon, to name just a few.

Two downstairs theaters offer free films and lectures. Since one side of the museum is a wall of glass, the interior light is exquisite. Of course, visit the Sculpture Garden, with its abundance of sitting space and exquisite fountains and sculpture. Then go on to the Garden Cafe for a snack. The two-leveled museum store carries an enormous selection of books and gifts. MOMA is not just a museum; it's a consummate repository of high-level 20th-century art.

NEW YORK PUBLIC LIBRARY

OPEN:	*Mon., Tues., Wed. 10-7:30; Thurs., Fri., Sat. 10-6*	ENTRY:	*Free*
		TYPE:	*General*
		ADDRESS:	*5th Ave. at 42 St.*
CLOSED:	*Sunday*	TEL:	*212-930-0800*
SUB:	*IRT #7 to 42 St. IND D to 42 St.*	GIFT SHOP:	*Yes*
		CAFE:	*No*
BUS:	*M1, M2, M3 M4 to 42 St.*	KIDS:	*Yes*
		RATING:	★★★★

Climb up the broad steps under the watchful eyes of Patience and Fortitude, the two majestic lions guarding the entrance. This is not only a place where one may borrow any of eight million books, return it, and continue borrowing forever, but it's also the main branch of a system that covers five boroughs with 80 branches.

This immense Beaux Arts building contains a wealth of archives whose scope defies the imagination but includes rare books and manuscripts, illustrations, prints, engravings, and paintings. Its Great Reading Room alone is larger than most libraries. Do stop at the Celeste Bartos Forum, a gorgeous salon for lectures, concerts, and films. This is the only place I know of where one can secure a complete education absolutely free.

44

UPTOWN EAST

UPTOWN EAST

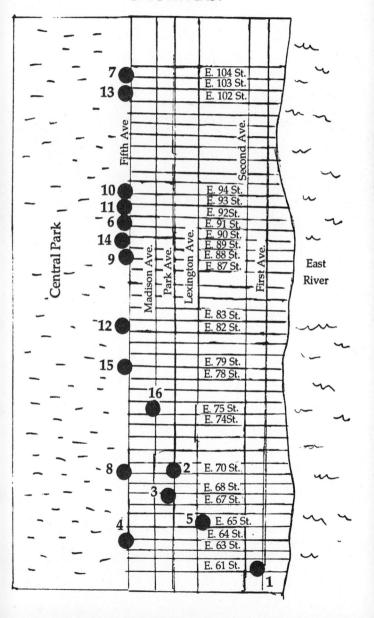

ABIGAIL ADAMS SMITH HOME

OPEN:	*Mon.-Fri. 12-4*	TYPE:	*Historical*
CLOSED:	*Sat., Sun.; month of August; Holidays*	ADDRESS:	*421 E. 61 St. at 2nd Ave.*
		TEL:	*212-838-6878*
SUB:	*IRT Lex to 59 St.*	GIFT SHOP:	*Yes*
BUS:	*3rd Ave. to 61 St.*	CAFE:	*No*
ENTRY:	*Adult $3; Sr. & Student $1*	KIDS:	*No*
		RATING:	★★★

Abigail Adams Smith was the daughter of John and Abigail Adams and the sister of John Quincy Adams. Picture her nine-room stone carriage house, built in 1799 and now under the shadow of the Queensboro Bridge, surrounded by New York's East Side's clatter and clutter.

It's a secluded little gem filled with original furnishings, arts, and memorabilia from the late 18th century: a charming colonial kitchen, a spinning wheel, and just plain simple, elegant decor.

Odd, isn't it, that Abigail Adams Smith never lived here? During summer months, the museum remains open on Tuesday evenings until 8 p.m. for concerts or craft demonstrations in the tranquil gardens, a bargain for an extra $3 admission. Refreshments will be served.

ASIA SOCIETY GALLERY

OPEN:	*Tues.-Sat. 11-6; Sun. 12-5*
CLOSED:	*Monday*
SUB:	*IRT Lex 3,4 to 68 St.*
BUS:	*2nd Ave. to 70 St.*
ENTRY:	*Adult $2; Sr. & Student $1*
TYPE:	*Ethnic*
ADDRESS:	*725 Park Ave.*
TEL:	*212-288-6400*
GIFT SHOP:	*Yes*
CAFE:	*No*
KIDS:	*Yes*
RATING:	★★★

The Asia Society building, in striking contrast to its Park Avenue apartment-house neighborhood, is of two-tone red granite, with clean lines. Its purpose is twofold. First, it houses the Society's offices and visiting exhibitions, and second, it displays the private and permanent collection of the John D. Rockefellers, which is the core of what's here, and handsome it is. Mr. Rockefeller, an astute collector, gathered these Asian treasures with loving devotion, and in the process achieved total perfection.

Eminent speakers appear, photographic exhibits and Asian films are shown, and dance performances are regularly given in the lower-level theater. Inquire at the main reception desk for the schedule of bus transportation to and from the Noguchi sculpture museum and gardens in Queens. After you've seen the gallery, allow yourself a few extra moments to visit the terrace, with its graceful and soothing fountains . Then it's back to the outside world.

CENTER FOR AFRICAN ART

OPEN:	*Tues.-Fri. 10-5; Sat. 11-5; Sun. 12-5*	TYPE:	*Ethnic*
		ADDRESS:	*54 E. 68 St.*
CLOSED:	*Monday & Holidays*	TEL:	*212-861-1200*
		GIFT SHOP:	*Yes*
SUB:	*IRT Lex to 68 St.*	CAFE:	*No*
BUS:	*Lex Ave. to 65 St.*	KIDS:	*Yes*
ENTRY:	*Voluntary contribution: Suggested adult $2.50; Sr. & Student $1.50*	RATING:	★★★

The museum is housed in a small Victorian mansion, unusual for New York's Upper East Side. When the Museum of Primitive Art merged into the Rockefeller Wing of the Metropolitan, New York was left without a center for African art. Now, this brand new Center has been designed and dedicated to increasing the understanding and appreciation of Africa's ancient cultures through well-researched, well-planned, and well-executed presentations.

The interior, updated to accommodate the Center's specific needs, is nicely done. Three exhibitions a year are held, for which the Center publishes its own catalogs and brochures. It also sponsors related lectures, slide shows, and film programs. Books on African art are sold on the main floor. If the current shows are any indication of this small museum's quality, it is guaranteed to be a success.

CENTRAL PARK ZOO

OPEN:	*Year round: Mon.-Fri. 10-5; Sat., Sun. & Holidays 10-5:30; Tues. eves. 10-8*	ENTRY:	*Adult $1; Sr. & Student .50*
		TYPE:	*Zoological*
		ADDRESS:	*5th Ave. at 64 St.*
		TEL:	*212-360-8213*
		GIFT SHOP:	*Yes*
SUB:	*IRT Lex to 68 St.*	CAFE:	*Yes*
BUS:	*Madison Ave. to 64 St.*	KIDS:	*Yes*
		RATING:	★★★★

You must admit that finding a zoo in the middle of New York City is rather unusual. This is a brand new one, and thanks to the New York Zoological Society, proves that you don't need to be big to be good. The zoo is divided into ten different areas and three major climate zones: Tropical, temperate, and polar. Appropriate animals are placed within their respective sectors.

Walk leisurely through the animals' naturalistic environments, up and around the landscape of the park. It's a beautifully designed setting, from the elegant arcade and central garden down to the sea lion pool. Have lunch in the garden cafe. The Children's Zoo, just next door, is an extra treat at only 10¢ admission for all.

CHINA INSTITUTE IN AMERICA

OPEN:	*Mon.-Fri. 9-5;*	ENTRY:	*Donations*
	Sat. 12-5	TYPE:	*Ethnic*
	(only during	ADDRESS:	*125 E. 65 St.*
	exhibitions)	TEL:	*212-744-8181*
SUB:	*IRT Lex to 68 St.*	GIFT SHOP:	*Yes*
BUS:	*2nd Ave. to 63*	CAFE:	*No*
	St. 3rd Ave. to	KIDS:	*No*
	63 St.	RATING:	*★★★*

The museum is called The China House Gallery. It's set in one room of a townhouse of the China Institute, its parent organization. The Institute promotes the U.S.-China relationship via art, painting, film series, and history and language classes, and it has advanced our knowledge and appreciation of China's history and culture.

The China Institute also succeeds in providing support groups and career building services for the Chinese-American community. Tours to Japan, China, and Thailand are offered, and the School of Chinese Studies is well attended. There are two principal shows held yearly; each is devoted exclusively to Chinese art. After your tour of the Gallery, be sure to walk through the Institute.

COOPER-HEWITT MUSEUM (SMITHSONIAN)

OPEN:	Wed.-Sat. 10-5; Tues. 10-9; Sun. 12-5	ENTRY:	Adult $3; Sr. & Student $1.50
CLOSED:	Monday & Holidays	TYPE:	Fine Arts
		ADDRESS:	2 E. 91 St.
SUB:	IRT Lex to 86 St.	TEL:	212-860-6868
BUS:	5th or Madison Ave. to 86 St.	GIFT SHOP:	Yes
		CAFE:	No
		KIDS:	Yes
		RATING:	★★★★

Millionnaire Andrew Carnegie had this 64-room mansion custom built in 1901, lived in it with his family, and conducted his business affairs here. It's spacious, baronial, and comfortable. But what better setting for the likes of an important museum for decorative arts and the designs of cities, landscapes, theaters, and buildings, not to mention fine arts, glass, and ceramics.

The Cooper-Hewitt's galleries cover assorted designs for every historical period over a span of 3,000 years. The museum was dormant for a number of years but is now enjoying a renaissance. The changing exhibitions really give Cooper-Hewitt its magnetism; they are excellent, and why not—it's part of the Smithsonian. The library alone is worth the visit.

EL MUSEO DEL BARRIO

OPEN:	*Wed.-Sun. 11-5*	**TYPE:**	*Ethnic*
CLOSED:	*Mon. & Tues.*	**ADDRESS:**	*1230 5th Ave.*
SUB:	*IRT Lex to 103 St.*		*at 104 St.*
BUS:	*Madison Ave.*	**TEL:**	*212-831-7272*
	to 104 St.	**GIFT SHOP:**	*No*
ENTRY:	*Suggested:*	**CAFE:**	*No*
	Adult $2; Sr. &	**KIDS:**	*Yes*
	Student $1	**RATING:**	★★★

This is the only museum in the country dedicated to the arts and culture of Mexico, Puerto Rico, South and Central America, and the Caribbean. It's also a distinguished Latin American cultural institution. It was organized in 1969 by a group of Puerto Rican parents to bring to their people a sense of Hispanic ancestry through the arts. They have succeeded.

The Hispanic community in New York has responded overwhelmingly. Not only have artists, writers, sculptors, and filmmakers respectfully submitted their works for viewing but people from all parts of New York now gravitate to this center for Latin American folk music, concerts, festivals, competitions, changing exhibitions, lectures, and public-education classes. The organizers and their entire community deserve kudos.

FRICK COLLECTION

OPEN:	*Tues.-Sat. 10-6; Sun. 1-6*	**TYPE:**	*Fine Arts*
CLOSED:	*Monday & Holidays*	**ADDRESS:**	*1E. 70 St. at 5th Ave.*
SUB:	*IRT Lex #6 to 68 St.*	**TEL:**	*212-288-0700*
BUS:	*M1, M2, M3, M4 to 68 St.*	**GIFT SHOP:**	*Yes*
		CAFE:	*No*
ENTRY:	*Adult $3; Sr. & Student $2*	**KIDS:**	*Yes*
		RATING:	★★★★

As its name implies, this was the home of the Frick family. It's where they lived, worked, and entertained. To shed some light on the background of this mansion, Henry Frick was a notorious, swashbuckling industrialist millionaire with exceptionally good taste in the fine arts. It was he who amassed this spectacular collection of breathtaking artistry. If you're curious about his appearance, his portrait hangs in the library.

But it's not only the works of art that lend the feeling of sensuality here; it's the decorative arts surrounding them—the walls, ceilings, carpets, and other accoutrements. The inner courtyard, with its delicate fountains, completes the sensation of total gratification. The Frick is a major museum attraction in New York. It will take your breath away. Don't miss it.

GUGGENHEIM MUSEUM

OPEN:	*Wed.-Sun. 1-5;* *Tues. 11-8*	ENTRY:	*Adult $4; Sr. &* *Student $3*
CLOSED:	*Monday,* *Christmas, New* *Year's Day*	TYPE:	*Fine Arts*
		ADDRESS:	*1071 5th Ave.* *at 88 St.*
SUB:	*IRT Lex to* *86 St.*	TEL:	*212-360-3513*
		GIFT SHOP:	*Yes*
BUS:	*Madison Ave.* *to 86 St.*	CAFE:	*No*
		KIDS:	*Yes*
		RATING:	★★★★

You probably know that Frank Lloyd Wright designed this building but did you also know that it's his only work in New York City? And it's not only what's being shown here but what it's being shown *in* that draws the huge crowds. Alas, Mr. Wright did not live to see its opening in 1959.

The museum owns about 180 canvases of Kandinsky, scores of Chagalls, and numerous works by Impressionists, Post-Impressionists, the School of Paris, etc., and there are more Cézannes here than in Paris. To accommodate Mr. Wright's architecture, visitors start at the top of the museum and view art as they descend its seven circular levels to the main floor below.

The museum shop has some of the most unique and exciting gifts of any museum, including eclectic jewelry and small Calder mobiles. You don't have to be a fan of Modern Art to love the Guggenheim—just relax and enjoy the show. Call first, please. At this writing, the museum is closed for renovation until 1993.

INTERNATIONAL CENTER OF PHOTOGRAPHY

OPEN:	*Wed.-Fri. 12-5; Sat., Sun. 11-6; Tues. 12-8*	ENTRY:	*Adult $3; Sr. & Student $1.50*
CLOSED:	*Monday & Holidays*	TYPE:	*Media*
		ADDRESS:	*1130 5th Ave. at 94 St.*
SUB:	*IRT Lex to 96 St.*	TEL:	*212-860-1777*
BUS:	*Madison Ave. to 96 St.*	GIFT SHOP:	*Yes*
		CAFE:	*No*
		KIDS:	*Yes*
		RATING:	★★★★

The museum is devoted exclusively to the techniques and styles of photographers and photography. Collections, programs, and publications embrace the universe of the camera. Exhibiting participants exemplify camera artistry through landscapes, still lifes, portraits, and figures, and the viewer is bestowed with an aura of privilege.

Galleries contain extraordinary photography, and the list of masters is more than impressive: Capa, White, Cartier-Bresson, Feininger, Atget, Arbus, Steiglitz, Weston, all are here in imposing grandeur. Aside from lecture series and workshops, accredited Master of Arts programs are offered.

The basement is occupied by darkrooms, finishing rooms, a gallery for attending students, and a screening room. If you're searching for a thrilling museum, ICP is for you. Ah, the power of the picture.

JEWISH MUSEUM

OPEN:	*Tues.-Fri. 10-3; Sun. 10-5*	**ENTRY:**	*Adult $5; Sr. & Student $2*
CLOSED:	*Sat., Mon. & Jewish Holidays*	**TYPE:**	*Ethnic*
		ADDRESS:	*5th Ave. at 92 St.*
SUB:	*IRT Lex to 96 St.*	**TEL:**	*212-724-1143*
BUS:	*Madison Ave. to 92 St.*	**GIFT SHOP:**	*Yes*
		CAFE:	*No*
		KIDS:	*Yes*
		RATING:	★★★★

The museum is under the auspices of the Jewish
Theological Seminary of America and dedicates itself to
illuminating Jewish art, culture, and tradition through arts,
artifacts and ceremonial objects, and the expression of
Jewish identity. Israeli artists are prevalent but Jewish
artists from other countries are given equal space. Much
of the collection was taken from pre-World War II
synagogues of Europe, when far-sighted Jewry realized
that, in order to preserve their legacy, they had better
move their precious objects out of Europe to the U.S.

The archaeological display sheds glowing light on
Israel's 4,000-year history. The tiny five-seat theater in the

corner of one room shows films pertaining to significant moments in Jewish history, and the Jewish experience is portrayed in movies, TV, and theater. Visit George Segal's poignant sculpture, The Holocaust, on the second floor. The museum carries an atmosphere of devotion seldom felt in other museums. I urge you to visit the Jewish Museum. But call first. The museum is temporarily residing in the New York Historical Society while their own building undergoes restoration until 1993.

METROPOLITAN MUSEUM OF ART

OPEN:	Sun.-Thurs. 9:30-5:15; Fri. & Sat. 9:30-8:45	ENTRY:	Adult $6; Sr. & Student $3
		TYPE:	Fine Arts
CLOSED:	Monday & Holidays	ADDRESS:	5th Ave. at 82 St.
SUB:	IRT Lex to 86 St.	TEL:	212-879-5500
		GIFT SHOP:	Yes
BUS:	Madison Ave. to 82 St.	CAFE:	Yes
		KIDS:	Yes
SUB:	IRT Lex. to 86 St.	RATING:	★★★★

It would be impossible to cite all that the Magnificent Met offers. The number of books written on it could fill a large library. It's one of the most celebrated institutions of art in the world, certainly the largest in the country, with dozens of separate sections, each one more astonishing than the last. Its private collection is so vast that only a small fraction of it can be displayed at one time. Everything you ever dreamed of seeing under one roof is here—it's simply mind-boggling.

Don't even think of doing the Met in one day; you couldn't cover everything in six. Notice upon entering the museum that each section has its own hours. If you plan on more than one visit, I strongly advise having a game plan for each. If not, you may find yourself wandering aimlessly; but that may not be too bad, either, considering where you are.

To give you an idea of the complexity and expense of running this massive operation, the Met staffs nearly 2,000 employees and budgets roughly $85 million a year. It also offers ten different types of membership plans. There are 32 acres of floor space and 21 separate gift shops; and the Met is constantly expanding, improving, and updating.

On Friday and Saturday evenings from 5 to 8, you are invited to enjoy a string quartet in the Great Hall Balcony, included in your admission. Cocktails are offered. Elevate on up to the roof garden, even briefly, for a spectacular view of New York. Lunch, brunch, or cocktails are served on the main floor. Don't forget the Junior Museum in the lower level. This amazing museum has proven that through intelligent planning and management, a museum can be not only self-supporting but successfully profitable.

MUSEUM OF THE CITY OF NEW YORK

OPEN:	Wed.-Sat. 10-5; Sun. 1-5; groups on Tuesday	ENTRY:	Adult $4; Sr. & Student $3
		TYPE:	Historical
CLOSED:	Monday & Holidays	ADDRESS:	1220 5th Ave. at 103 St.
		TEL:	212-534-1672
SUB:	IRT Lex to 103 St.	GIFT SHOP:	Yes
BUS:	Madison Ave. to 102 St.	CAFE:	No
		KIDS:	Yes
		RATING:	★★★

The main focus of this museum is its collection of paintings, maps, photographs, and documents pertaining to New York from its Dutch settlement in the early 1600s to its major role of today, presented through displays that are easy to follow and explanations that all can understand. Try to see the multi-media film "Big Apple," an exciting 20-minute jazzy run through New York's past.

The gift shop, one of the most comprehensive I've seen in New York, sells an extensive assortment of books and memorabilia on the history of the five boroughs. I still can't imagine why there are two fully furnished rooms on the fifth floor, belonging to Mr. Nelson Rockefeller, who held office as New York's governor. On your way out, glance at the display of New York before the Europeans arrived. If you've ever lived or wanted to live in New York, no matter for how long, visit this museum.

NATIONAL ACADEMY OF DESIGN

OPEN:	*Wed.-Sun. 12-5; Tues. 12-8*	**TYPE:**	*Fine Arts*
CLOSED:	*Monday & Holidays*	**ADDRESS:**	*1083 5th Ave. at 89 St.*
SUB:	*IRT Lex #4,5,6 to 86 St.*	**TEL:**	*212-369-4880*
		GIFT SHOP:	*Yes*
BUS:	*M1, M2, M3 to 86 St.*	**CAFE:**	*No*
		KIDS:	*Yes*
ENTRY:	*Adult $3.50; Sr. & Student $2*	**RATING:**	★★★★

The museum's function is threefold: It is a museum, an honorary society of artists, and a school of fine arts, all highly prestigious. The patrician townhouse has four floors filled with paintings, sculptures, drawings, arts and architecture, a grand winding staircase with the goddess Diana at its base, and elegant galleries. The museum maintains a legendary membership roster that is enviable for its major masters and distinguished designers, all of whom must submit a self-portrait for entry and samples of their most prized works.

Aside from this permanent collection, there's a wealth of Renaissance treasures. The changing exhibitions can be described as matchless. The gift shop offers a most unusual and varied collection of art books and cards. I highly recommend the Academy: It's rarely visited, yet it's one of New York's best.

UKRAINIAN INSTITUTE

OPEN:	*Tues. 9:30-5; Sat. 9:30-8:45 only during exhibitions; otherwise by appointment*	ENTRY:	*Voluntary donation*
		TYPE:	*Ethnic*
		ADDRESS:	*2 E. 79 St.*
		TEL:	*212-288-8660*
		GIFT SHOP:	*No*
SUB:	*IRT Lex #4,5,6 to 77 St.*	CAFE:	*No*
		KIDS:	*No*
BUS:	*5th or Madison Ave. to 77 St.*	RATING:	★★★

The mansion's striking architecture stands out along Fifth Avenue's Museum Mile. Designed in 1900 as a private villa, purchased and renamed in the 1950s by the Society's founder, it's now a National Historical Landmark.

The aim of the Ukraine Society is to develop, sponsor, and promote Ukranian activities and to acquaint the public with the Ukraine's culture, history, art, and music through films, concerts, lectures, and classes. It's also a research center, with archives and documents pertaining to the 20th-century Ukraine. There's a permanent costume display and religious and folk art displays. The Institute hosts temporary exhibitions, showing prominent artists from the Ukraine.

WHITNEY MUSEUM

OPEN:	Wed.-Sat.11-5; Tues. 1-8; Sun. 12-6	ENTRY:	Adult $5; Sr. & Student $3
		TYPE:	Fine Arts
CLOSED:	Monday & Holidays	ADDRESS:	945 Madison Ave. at 75 St.
SUB:	IRT Lex #4,5,6 to 77 St.	TEL:	212-570-3676
		GIFT SHOP:	Yes
BUS:	M1, M2, M3, M4 to 77 St.	CAFE:	Yes
		KIDS:	Yes
		RATING:	★★★★

The Whitney concentrates on the unique and extraordinary in modern American art and remains one of the world's foremost repositories for 20th-century art. Gertrude Vanderbilt Whitney, a sculptress and art collector, created the museum in 1930, and the majority of the permanent collection consists of her acquisitions.

Changing exhibitions and special events are first class, and educational programs are more than successful. The permanent collection soars in its greatness. For some reason the restaurant enjoys immense popularity. Odd for a museum, but the food is just plain good.

Whitney has three public branch museums: Equitable Center, 7th Ave. and 51st; Philip Morris Center, 42nd and Park Ave.; and Federal Reserve Plaza, Maiden Lane. All are free and superb. You get more than your money's worth at the Whitney.

UPTOWN WEST

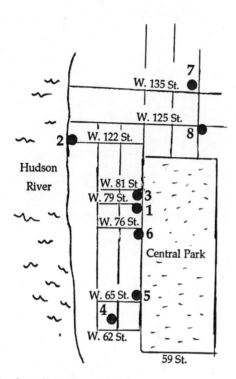

1. American Museum of Natural History, p. 72
2. General Grant's Tomb, p. 73
3. Hayden Planetarium, p. 75
4. Lincoln Center for the Performing Arts, p. 76
5. Museum of American Folk Art, p. 78
6. New York Historical Society, p. 79
7. Schomberg Center for Research in Black Culture, p. 80
8. Studio Museum in Harlem, p. 81

AMERICAN MUSEUM OF NATURAL HISTORY

OPEN:	*Mon.-Thurs. 10-5:45; Fri., Sat. 10-9; Sun. 10-5:45*	**ENTRY:**	*Adult $5; Sr. & Student $2.50*
CLOSED:	*Major Holidays*	**TYPE:**	*Science*
SUB:	*IND C or K to 81 St.*	**ADDRESS:**	*Central Pk. West at 79 St.*
BUS:	*M7, M10 to 81 St.*	**TEL:**	*212-769-5100*
		GIFT SHOP:	*Yes*
		CAFE:	*Yes*
		KIDS:	*Yes*
		RATING:	★★★★

The museum, the largest of its kind in the world, occupies four city blocks and 22 buildings, with an incredible range of objects in the natural sciences, anthropology, biology, paleontology, zoology, and mineralogy. To avoid being overwhelmed, pick up a free brochure and decide on the subjects you prefer.

I recommend the Akeley Hall of African Mammals, main floor; the Hall of Ocean Life, main floor; and the Halls of Early and Late Dinosaurs, fourth floor. Or, drop into the NatureMax Theater, main floor, for "The Earth and Its Creatures," a film with explosive impact. One shortcoming, however, is the need for improved lighting in the older, more remote sections of the museum.

GENERAL GRANT'S TOMB

OPEN:	*Wed.-Sun. 9-5*	TYPE:	*Historical*
CLOSED:	*Mon., Tues. &*	ADDRESS:	*Riverside Drive*
	National		*at 122 St.*
	Holidays	TEL:	*212-666-1640*
SUB:	*IRT #1 to*	GIFT SHOP:	*Yes*
	116 St.	CAFE:	*No*
BUS:	*5th Ave. to*	KIDS:	*Yes*
	116 St.	RATING:	*★★★*
ENTRY:	*Voluntary*		
	donation		

Ulysses S. Grant, Civil War hero and two-term president of the United States, was a rather quiet man and not widely understood. The museum is his mausoleum, fashioned after Napoleon's tomb in Paris. Grant's life is portrayed in photographs, portraits, documents, and drawings. Notice that one of his close friends was Mark Twain.

Grant was greatly admired by the black community, and in 1868 it was that portion of the voters that decided his election to the presidency. Those three immense mosaic murals show General Grant as the central figure in three major Civil War battles: Vicksburg, Chattanooga, and Appomattox.

After his presidency, Grant and his wife received international acclaim on a worldwide goodwill tour. In 1885 Grant died, a mere 63 years old. He left behind not only an illustrious career but a monumental work—his personal memoirs, completed one week before his death.

HAYDEN PLANETARIUM

OPEN:	*Mon.-Fri. 12-4:45;*	TYPE:	*Science*
	Sat. 10-5:45;	ADDRESS:	*Central Pk.*
	Sun. 12-5:45		*West at 81 St.*
CLOSED:	*Major Holidays*	TEL:	*212-769-5920*
BUS:	*M7, M10 to 81 St.*	GIFT SHOP:	*Yes*
SUB:	*IND C,K to 81 St.*	CAFE:	*Yes*
ENTRY:	*Adult $4; Sr. &*	KIDS:	*Yes*
	Student $3	RATING:	★★★★

Have you ever wondered why the sky is blue? Or what makes a rainbow? Well, the solutions are found here, along with many other answers about heavenly phenomena and wonders of the universe. The Hayden is actually the astronomy department of the American Museum of Natural History.

The "star" attraction is upstairs in the Sky Theater, with its huge domed ceiling and chairs that recline to almost a lying-down position, the better to see the star-studded ceiling show. The Hall of the Sun, also upstairs, has exhibits about that most perplexing celestial body. The Guggenheim Theater on the main floor shows films with vivid sound effects in the 360° room. There are exhibits on astronomy, space science, the moon, the planets, the subject of extraterrestrial life, meteors, minerals, and gems. Be prepared for groups of children, which means a high excitement level.

LINCOLN CENTER FOR THE PERFORMING ARTS

OPEN:	*Lincoln Center complex is open year round daily. Library & Museum of the Performing Arts: Mon. & Thurs. 12-8; Wed. & Fri; 12-6; Sat. 10-6*	SUB:	*IRT B'way. #1 to 66 St.*
		BUS:	*M5,7; M104*
		ENTRY:	*Free*
		TYPE:	*Miscellaneous*
		ADDRESS:	*B'way. at 65 St.*
		TEL:	*212-870-1630*
		GIFT SHOP:	*Yes*
		CAFE:	*Yes*
		KIDS:	*Yes*
CLOSED:	*Tuesday & Sunday*	RATING:	★★★★

Because music, theater, and dance are part of the arts, and because Lincoln Center is dedicated to the perpetuation of these forms, I've included this stunning complex, completed in 1969, as a significant section of this book. The architectural design is a splendid sight to behold. There are six buildings: New York State Theater, Metropolitan Opera House, Juilliard School and Alice Tully Hall, Vivian Beaumont Theater, Public Library and Museum of the Performing Arts, and Avery Fisher Hall.

Although each conducts its own programs and activities, all operate closely to and with one another.

Broadcasts, telecasts, festivals, competitions, and community programs share the spotlight. Future plans for an ambitious enlargement, including a 25-story building, will increase Lincoln Center's space. Take a one-hour guided tour, and as long as you're here, stop in at the extraordinary Museum of the Performing Arts. I promise you no regrets.

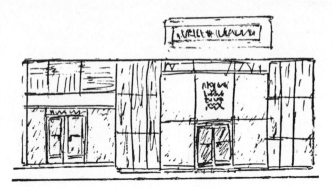

MUSEUM OF AMERICAN FOLK ART

OPEN:	*Daily year round, 9-9*	ENTRY:	*Free*
		TYPE:	*General*
ADDRESS:	*Columbus Ave. between 65 St. & 66 St.*	TEL:	*212-977-7298*
		GIFT SHOP:	*Yes*
		CAFE:	*No*
SUB:	*IRT 7th Ave. #1,2,3 to 66 St. Lincoln Center*	KIDS:	*Yes*
		RATING:	★★★

This branch of the Folk Art museum opened in 1989 and will serve as headquarters until the museum's permanent home on West 53rd Street opens about 1993. You can't miss it—there's Lincoln Center just across the street. The museum's structural design is unusual: Four wings radiate from a central sky-lit atrium and garden court. This bright and light public area serves as a backdrop for the large-scale, enchanting folk sculptures.

Each year four exhibitions of folk art and quilt festivals are held, with an occasional one-man show. Within the last ten years there has been a resurgence of interest in folk art, and devotees are ecstatic about its long overdue recognition. There's a refreshing charm and universal appeal here. Naive art is truly a welcome respite from today's tense, high-tech pace. Stop in at the gift shop just next door for books and one-of-a-kind handcrafted items.

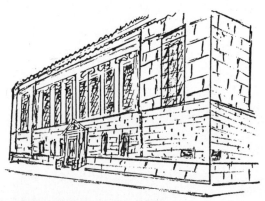

NEW YORK HISTORICAL SOCIETY

OPEN:	*Tues.-Sun. 10-5*	TYPE:	*Historical*
CLOSED:	*Monday & Holidays*	ADDRESS:	*170 Central Pk. West*
SUB:	*IND B,C,K to 81 St.*	TEL:	*212-873-3400*
		GIFT SHOP:	*Yes*
BUS:	*M7, M10, M11 to 76 St.*	CAFE:	*No*
		KIDS:	*Yes*
ENTRY:	*Adult $4.50; Sr. & Student $3*	RATING:	★★★

This 19th-century Beaux Arts granite building is an austere reminder of yesterday's grand, then Upper West Side. It's a combination museum and research library.

Special attractions are the Silver Gallery, John James Audubon watercolor illustrations, 17th- and 18th-century period rooms, and a glittering display of Tiffany glass and lamps. The upper floor holds a wealth of information on the urban and suburban landscape of New York, fine painting and portrait galleries, and a library with priceless manuscripts, documents, and books. This is a treasure house. You might glimpse the wall map of the British Empire in America, c. 1733.

The museum store must be visited. Everything you always wanted to know about New York is inside.

SCHOMBERG CENTER FOR RESEARCH IN BLACK CULTURE

OPEN:	Mon., Tues., Wed. 12-8; Fri., Sat. 10-6	**ENTRY:**	Free
		TYPE:	Ethnic
CLOSED:	Thurs., Sun. & Holidays	**ADDRESS:**	515 Lenox Ave. at 135 St.
		TEL:	212-491-2200
SUB:	IRT 7th Ave. #2, 3 to 135 St.	**GIFT SHOP:**	Yes
		CAFE:	No
BUS:	M7, M100 to 135 St.	**KIDS:**	Yes
		RATING:	★★★

This is an important, scholarly research center and a branch of the New York Public Library, with reference rooms, archives, and large galleries. It was founded by Arthur Schomberg, a Puerto Rican of African descent. The center contains about a million volumes by or about Africans and Afro-Americans in addition to periodicals, pamphlets, manuscripts, prints and drawings, photographs, paintings, sculpture, sheet music, recorded music, posters, and playbills. It's the world's most comprehensive documentation of blacks, rich in history, folklore, and the roots of the black experience.

Located in the heart of Harlem, the library is a reminder of a spiritual legacy handed down to us by generations of a wounded, but gifted, community. It's also about a half-mile from the Studio Museum in Harlem.

STUDIO MUSEUM IN HARLEM

OPEN:	*Wed.-Fri. 10-5; Sat., Sun. 1-6*	TYPE:	*Ethnic*
CLOSED:	*Mon. & Tues.*	ADDRESS:	*144 W. 125 St.*
SUB:	*IRT 7th Ave. #2,3 to 125 St.*	TEL:	*212-864-4500*
		GIFT SHOP:	*Yes*
BUS:	*M2, M7, M100 to 125 St.*	CAFE:	*No*
		KIDS:	*Yes*
ENTRY:	*Adult $2; Sr. & Student $1*	RATING:	★★★

This excellent museum is devoted solely to African, Afro-American, and Caribbean artists and is home to treasures of black art and artifacts. It opened during the height of the Civil Rights Movement in 1968 and has grown and developed into an elegant, sophisticated cultural institution. The permanent collection of paintings, prints, sculptures, weaving, and photographs is superior.

Changing exhibits present arts of black America and the African diaspora through the eyes and hands of eminent artists. Workshops, tours, films, educational programs, seminars, and classes are held here, as is an artist-in-residence program. The historic photographic essay of Harlem in its heyday by James Van Der Zee shouldn't be missed. The museum's goal for a sculpture garden is close to fulfillment. Studio Museum in Harlem is on its way to becoming one of the world's leading art centers for the black community.

WASHINGTON HEIGHTS

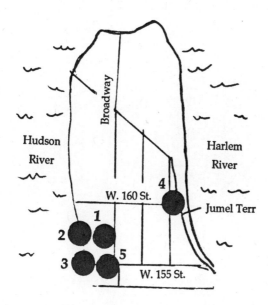

1. American Academy of Arts and Letters, p. 84
2. American Numismatic Society, p. 86
3. Hispanic Society of America, p. 87
4. Morris-Jumel Mansion, p. 88
5. Museum of the American Indian, p. 89

AMERICAN ACADEMY OF ARTS AND LETTERS

OPEN:	*During exhibitions only: March; May/June; Nov./Dec. Tues.-Sun. 1-4*	**TYPE:**	*General*
		ADDRESS:	*Audubon Terrace, Broadway & 155 St.*
SUB:	*IRT #1 to 157 St. & B'way.*	**TEL:**	*212-368-5900*
		GIFT SHOP:	*No*
BUS:	*M4, M5 to 156 St.*	**CAFE:**	*No*
		KIDS:	*No*
ENTRY:	*Free*	**RATING:**	★★★

The Academy is an organization formed for the recognition of persons of special distinction in literature and the arts, architecture, poetry, music, and a dozen or more recipients of fellowships and memorial awards. Membership in the Academy consists of eminent artists, musicians, and writers from both the United States and foreign countries. The membership list is more than impressive, and to be invited to join the Academy is considered recognition of the highest artistic merit.

Three exhibitions a year are held during March, May/June, and November/December. The galleries are open to the public only during those times, and visitors must call first. The Academy is housed in two buildings with elegant appointments and fine paintings appropriate to this particular component of artistic aristocracy. Although the neighborhood is not attractive, it might behoove you to make the trip.

AMERICAN NUMISMATIC SOCIETY

OPEN:	*Tues.-Sat. 9-4:30; Sun. 1-4*	TYPE:	*Miscellaneous*
		ADDRESS:	*Audubon Terrace, B'way. at 155 St.*
CLOSED:	*Monday & Holidays*		
SUB:	*B'way. #1 to 157 St and B'way.*	TEL:	*212-234-3130*
		GIFT SHOP:	*No*
		CAFE:	*No*
BUS:	*M4, M5 to 156 St.*	KIDS:	*No*
		RATING:	★★
ENTRY:	*Free*		

Numismatics is the study of coins, currency, and medals as they relate to history, archaeology, and economics. The museum is composed of two rooms. The first tells the story of the development of coins from the pre-Christian era until today. The second is devoted to decorations and medals of honor, covering the broad expanse of thousands of years and dozens of countries, including commemorative coins of historic events.

Not only is their library endowed with a comprehensive collection of periodicals and catalogs but there is a large group of serious students and collectors who maintain diligent interest in the Society.

HISPANIC SOCIETY OF AMERICA

OPEN:	*Tues.-Sat. 8-4; Sun. 1-4*	TYPE:	*Ethnic*
CLOSED:	*Monday & Holidays*	ADDRESS:	*Audubon Terrace, B'way. at 155 St.*
SUB:	*B'way. #1 to 157 St. & B'way*	TEL:	*212-926-2234*
BUS:	*M4, M5 to 156 St.*	GIFT SHOP:	*Yes*
		CAFE:	*No*
		KIDS:	*Yes*
ENTRY:	*Donation*	RATING:	★★

One might imagine that the word "Hispanic" would suggest a presentation of present-day social history. That, however, is not the case. All contents pertain to Iberian (Spanish/Portugese) literature, sculpture, paintings, ceramics, and decorative arts dating from Roman/Moorish times.

After entering, go up to the first floor. The main gallery with its high ceiling and balcony overlooking a solemn two-story salon encircled by sculptured archways is truly grand. Early Mediterranean arts and hand-set mosaic portions of rooms are voluptuous. The only problem is that not all exhibits are dated. The viewer is therefore left to his or her own devices. The library holds thousands of volumes, maps, and historic manuscripts. Did you notice the ancient Hebrew Bible? Top off your visit with a glance at the El Greco, Goya, and Velasquez paintings.

MORRIS-JUMEL MANSION

OPEN:	*Tues.-Sun. 10-4*	ENTRY:	*Adult $2; Sr. &*
CLOSED:	*Monday &*		*Student $1*
	Holidays	TYPE:	*Historical*
SUB:	*IND A to 125*	ADDRESS:	*1765 Jumel*
	St., local B to		*Terr.*
	163 St.	TEL:	*212-923-8008*
BUS:	*#2,3, Madison*	GIFT SHOP:	*Yes*
	Ave. to St.	CAFE:	*No*
	Nicholas &	KIDS:	*No*
	160 St.	RATING:	★★

Not only is this Georgian residence situated atop the highest spot in New York City but it is one of only a half-dozen mansion/villa museums remaining from the 18th and 19th centuries (Abigail Adams Smith's and Teddy Roosevelt's residences are two others). The museum holds some great historic memories. Firstly, Aaron Burr was married here to Mme. Jumel. Secondly, the mansion's claim to having served briefly as George Washington's headquarters in 1776 is perfectly true. In addition, the villa was used during the 1780s as military governing chambers. Federal/Empire period furnishings are intact; charming flowered wallpaper is in some rooms, Napoleonic design in others; and the octagonal drawing room is tastefully elegant. What a pleasure to visit one of the last vestiges of Old New York!

MUSEUM OF THE AMERICAN INDIAN

OPEN: *Tues.-Sat. 10-5; Sun. 1-5*	**TYPE:** *Ethnic*
CLOSED: *Monday & Holidays*	**ADDRESS:** *Audubon Terrace, B'way. at 155 St.*
SUB: *B'way. #1 to 157 St. & B'way.*	**TEL:** *212-283-2420*
BUS: *M4, M5 to 156 St.*	**GIFT SHOP:** *Yes*
ENTRY: *Adult $3; Sr. & Student $2; Native Americans free*	**CAFE:** *No*
	KIDS: *Yes*
	RATING: ★★★

The three-story museum has more than four million artifacts representing Native American culture of the Western Hemisphere. Names like Seminole, Navajo, Iroquois, Cherokee, Sitting Bull, Crazy Horse, and Geronimo are scattered about like jewels in a sea of beads and wampum. Masks and clothing, pottery and sculpture, superstitious images and spiritual animals, paintings and prints, and crafts are treasures one and all.

We have George Heye to thank for all this, the compulsive accumulator, who, at the turn of this century, swept through the Americas buying anything and everything he could fasten his acquisitive hands and money on, enabling us to celebrate the American Indian's influence on our civilization. The museum needs more space, and rumor has it that it might move.

INWOOD

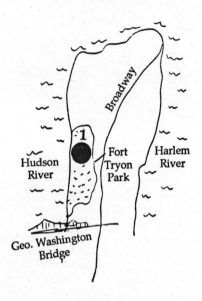

1. The Cloisters, p. 91

THE CLOISTERS

OPEN:	*Tues.-Sun. 9:30-5:15 (Mar.-Oct.); 9:30-4:45 (Nov.-Feb.)*	ENTRY:	*Voluntary contribution*
		TYPE:	*General*
		ADDRESS:	*Fort Tryon Park*
CLOSED:	*Monday & Holidays*	TEL:	*212-923-3700*
		GIFT SHOP:	*Yes*
SUB:	*IND 8th Ave. to 190 St.*	CAFE:	*No*
		KIDS:	*Yes*
BUS:	*M4 to Cloisters*	RATING:	★★★★

The Cloisters, an ecclesiastical setting high above the Hudson River at the north tip of Manhattan, is more than tranquil: It is ephemeral and immortal. Several medieval Romanesque and Gothic cloisters, monasteries, and gardens are all faithfully presented. The newly designed Treasury holds a spectacular collection of precious works of art, textiles, woods and ivories, liturgical objects, and gold and enameled pieces. Another treasure is the set of Unicorn Tapestries, similar to those in the Musée de Cluny in Paris.

Chapels hold paintings and altarpieces; galleries hold manuscripts, sculptures, and stained glass panels. Flower and herb gardens are of lovely simplicity. The Cloisters, a branch of the Metropolitam Museum of Art, provides a scholarly and beautiful glimpse back into the Middle Ages. On weekends during the summer, shuttle bus trips are offered from the Met.

QUEENS

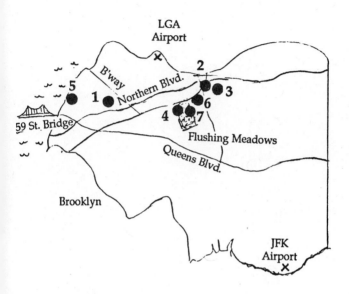

1. American Museum of the Moving Image, p. 94
2. Bowne House, p. 96
3. Kingsland House, p. 97
4. New York Hall of Science, p. 99
5. Noguchi Museum and Gardens, p. 100
6. Queens Botanical Gardens, p. 102
7. Queens Museum, p. 103

AMERICAN MUSEUM OF THE MOVING IMAGE

OPEN: *Tues.-Fri. 12-4; Sat., Sun. 12-6*	**TYPE:** *Media*
CLOSED: *Monday*	**ADDRESS:** *35th Ave. at 36 St., Astoria*
SUB: *B'way. R or IND G to Steinway St., Astoria*	**TEL:** *718-784-0077*
	GIFT SHOP: *Yes*
	CAFE: *No*
	KIDS: *Yes*
ENTRY: *Adult $5; Sr. & Student $2*	**RATING:** ★★★★

This museum is one of the most razzle-dazzle centers of art in New York. It's a gigantic attempt at demystifying mass entertainment and conveying the impact of TV and video on our culture and society. Why Queens? Well, Astoria enjoys the privilege of having been a major center for the entire East Coast during the heyday of film-making. Their presentations are close to perfection, their galleries are huge, and the movie theater will set you spinning.

Nothing has been left to chance. The technical displays are intricate and mind-boggling. Demonstrations of the moving image are fast paced and very visual. You could spend the entire day here and still not experience everything. The museum has established itself as a world-class exhibition center. Its displays are highly eclectic and inventive. Don't miss the Enchanted Mirror (second floor). On the way out, visit the extraordinary gift shop.

BOWNE HOUSE

OPEN:	*Tues., Sat., Sun. 2:30-4:30*	ENTRY:	*Adult $2; Child $1*
		TYPE:	*Historical*
CLOSED:	*Mid-Dec to mid-Jan*	ADDRESS:	*3701 Bowne St., Flushing*
SUB:	*IRT #7 to Main St., Flushing; Long Island Railroad to Flushing*	TEL:	*718-359-0528*
		GIFT SHOP:	*Yes*
		CAFE:	*No*
		KIDS:	*No*
		RATING:	★★★

John Bowne built this house in 1660 and it's probably the oldest building in New York. Its significance is not confined to its architectural quality, however, for it carries a more spiritual connotation. At that time Governor Peter Stuyvesant outlawed any and all religions not of the Dutch Church. Mr. Bowne, a Quaker, held meetings for worship, was arrested, imprisoned, and banished to Europe for two years, then returned to his family in Flushing. It is felt that as a direct result of this drama the gentle, modest Quakers were granted religious freedom, which eventually led to the adoption of the Constitution's First Amendment a century later.

Thanks to successive Bowne generations and the Queens Historical Society, Bowne House retains all its original furnishings and touching simplicity. A tour combines Bowne House, Kingsland House (next door), and the Quaker church, just a few steps away.

KINGSLAND HOUSE

OPEN:	Tues., Sat., Sun. 2:30-4:30	**ENTRY:**	*Suggested donation: Adult $2; Sr. & Student $1*
CLOSED:	Mon., Wed., Thurs., Fri., Holiday	**TYPE:**	*Historical*
SUB:	IRT #7 to Main St., Flushing; Long Island Railroad to Flushing	**ADDRESS:**	*143-55 37th Ave., Flushing*
		TEL:	*718-939-0647*
		GIFT SHOP:	*Yes*
		CAFE:	*No*
		KIDS:	*No*
		RATING:	★★★

Although Kingsland Homestead was built in 1742 by a wealthy Quaker farmer named Doughty, it derives its name from an English sea captain, Joseph King, who married Doughty's daughter and inherited the house. Its architecture is Revolutionary-Dutch-English style, with typically quadrant windows, gambrel roof, and central chimney.

Kingsland House features changing Victorian exhibitions. The Queens Historical Society's quarters are upstairs, and it is they who, along with the Kingsland

Preservation Committee, plan workshops, lectures, and historical exhibitions. On permanent display are Captain King's documents and rare books, photos of early Queens, and maps dating back to the mid-1850s. That enormous beech tree alongside the building, the oldest of its kind in the U.S., was planted around 1850 and is still growing. Bowne House, another historical prize, is just across the park.

NEW YORK HALL OF SCIENCE

OPEN:	*Wed.-Sun. 10-5*	ADDRESS:	*47-01 111 St.,*
CLOSED:	*Mon. & Tues.*		*Flushing*
SUB:	*IRT #7 to 111 St.*	TEL:	*718-699-0675*
		GIFT SHOP:	*Yes*
ENTRY:	*Adult $3; Sr. & Student $2*	CAFE:	*No*
		KIDS:	*Yes*
TYPE:	*Science*	RATING:	★★★

The Hall of Science is a science-technology center, with hands-on exhibits in light and color, structure, feedback, atoms, and micro-organisms—and it's a smash hit. Based on the premise that science is more fascinating with the help of human participation, all exhibits encompass and connect everyday reflexes such as hearing, motion, balance, and common sense to scientific phenomena with participatory help.

The museum is on the lower level. The upper portion is hollow, 80 feet high, of curved cement, with its walls inlaid in blue stained glass, and viewed from the inside it's pretty dazzling. The building's odd configuration was designed for the 1964 World's Fair by the very same architect who designed the Trylon and Perisphere for the 1939 World's Fair. The museum is crowded with visitors at all times, and the excitement (noise) level is very high. The Musical Rainfall exhibit is particularly popular.

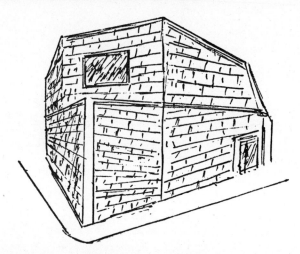

NOGUCHI MUSEUM AND GARDENS

OPEN:	*Wed. & Sat. 11-6, April to November*	ADDRESS:	*32-37 Vernon Blvd. at 33rd Rd., Astoria*
SUB:	*BMT RR Astoria to B'way.*	TEL:	*718-204-7088*
		GIFT SHOP:	*Yes*
ENTRY:	*Suggested donation: $2*	CAFE:	*No*
		KIDS:	*Yes*
TYPE:	*Fine Arts*	RATING:	★★★

It's nice to see an artist given the acknowledgments due him. Isamu Noguchi, who died in 1988, is considered a pure, innovative artist. His museum and gardens occupy a small triangular city block just under the 59th Street Queensborough Bridge on the Queens side. His works are intermingled within the museum's 12 galleries, each differing in style and material, and all sparkle with imposing power.

Outside, Noguchi's more recent chiseled granite boulders grace the gardens, dotted with bird baths and gurgling water basins. Noguchi designed stage settings for the Martha Graham Dance Company, sculptural pieces for Rockefeller Center in New York, a memorial bridge for

Hiroshima, a fountain on Fifth Avenue, a park in Miami, a marble sculpture for Venice, and more. I searched the museum to find models of those artistic masterpieces, but, unfortunately, they either do not exist or are not here. There's a noticeably calming influence both in the museum and the gardens. Noguchi's simplicity glows.

QUEENS BOTANICAL GARDENS

OPEN:	*Daily year round, 10-5*	TYPE:	*Botanical*
CLOSED:	*Month of March*	ADDRESS:	*43-50 Main St., Flushing*
SUB:	*IRT #7 to Main St., transfer to Q44 bus to Gardens*	TEL:	*718-886-3800*
		GIFT SHOP:	*Yes*
		CAFE:	*No*
		KIDS:	*Yes*
ENTRY:	*Free*	RATING:	★★★

Here's a bit of the country amid the clatter, clamor, and congestion of Flushing. Created only 25 years ago, these gardens are proof that it is possible to enjoy a variety of foliage without leaving town. Individual gardens are harmoniously designed, and tiny walks lead to tinkling waterfalls and rocky grottoes.

There's a Bird Garden, an Herb Garden, a Bee Garden, a Fountain Garden, and, of course, a Rose Garden. The Victorian Wedding Garden is reserved for ceremonies and photographs. The most desirable time of year to visit is the fall, when foliage is at its peak with blazing scarlets and yellows. It's not the largest botanical garden in New York, but one can sit on any bench and do nothing but admire flora and listen to birds.

QUEENS MUSEUM

OPEN:	*Tues.-Fri. 10-5; Sat. & Sun. 12-5*	TYPE:	*Fine Arts*
CLOSED:	*Monday & Holidays*	ADDRESS:	*NYC Building, Flushing Meadows*
SUB:	*IRT #7 to Willets Pt.*	TEL:	*718-592-5555*
		GIFT SHOP:	*Yes*
BUS:	*Q48 to Willets Pt.*	CAFE:	*No*
ENTRY:	*Adult $2; Sr. & Student $1*	KIDS:	*Yes*
		RATING:	★★★

The building was constructed to house the New York City Exhibit for the l939 World's Fair. You can't miss it: It's just next door to the still-standing Unisphere. Between then and now it has hosted the UN General Assembly (1946-50) and the second New York World's Fair in 1964. On permanent display is "The Heroic Spirit," a stunning sculpture gallery. Another attraction is "Panorama, " an immense scale model of New York's five boroughs.

The museum's Contemporary Gallery features temporary exhibitions covering almost all of art's epochs from the 18th century to contemporary. Visit the sculpture restoration studio in the basement. If you're lucky enough to be at this museum at the right time, you might catch the Tennis Open next door, a New York Mets ballgame across the lawn, or both. Also, weather permitting, you're directly under the take-off pattern for La Guardia Airport, a noisy attraction.

BROOKLYN

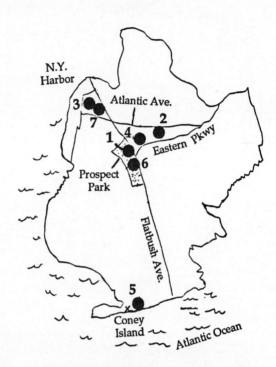

BROOKLYN BOTANICAL GARDENS

OPEN:	Tues.-Fri. 8-4:30; Sat., Sun. & Holidays 10-4:30	TYPE:	Botanical Gardens
CLOSED:	Monday	ADDRESS:	1000 Washington Ave.
SUB:	IRT 7th Ave. #2,3 to Eastern Pkwy.	TEL:	718-622-4433
ENTRY:	Voluntary donation	GIFT SHOP:	Yes
		CAFE:	Yes
		KIDS:	Yes
		RATING:	★★★★

The elegant Botanical Gardens, whose slogan is "Many Gardens Within a Garden," lives up to its reputation. Pick up a small booklet at the entrance for a complete diagram of the gardens. The new Steinhardt Conservatory with a $2 admission charge is worth every penny. It's a vision in superb glass architecture, with three separate pavilions in delicately tinted glass, a bonsai museum at one end, an aquatic greenhouse at the other, and a number of remarkable collections in between.

There are roughly 25 individual gardens, including the Cranford Rose Garden, the Herb Garden, and a Fragrance

Garden for the sight-impaired with Braille labels. The lily ponds, luscious trees, and rolling lawns contribute to a magical beauty equalling the grandeur of Monet's gardens in Giverny. The Brooklyn Museum is just next door.

BROOKLYN CHILDREN'S MUSEUM

OPEN:	Wed.,Thurs., Fri. 2-5; Sat., Sun., Holidays 12-5	ENTRY:	Adult $3; Sr., Student & Child $2
		TYPE:	General
CLOSED:	Mon. & Tues.	ADDRESS:	145 Brooklyn Ave.
SUB:	IRT #3 to Kingston- Eastern Pkwy.	TEL:	718-735-4400
		GIFT SHOP:	No
		CAFE:	No
BUS:	B7, B44, B47 to Museum	KIDS:	Yes
		RATING:	★★★

This unorthodox, imaginative museum is supposed to be participatory for kids, but from the corner of my eye at more than one exhibit I caught a glimpse of several adults with their hands on. It's a high-tech, gaily painted playground, and each presentation is smartly separated from the next so as not to confuse.

Upon entering, there's a stream within a "people tube," a wide drainage pipe that runs down the four levels of the museum, lit up in glorious fluorescent colors. Each level demonstrates the mysteries of the world: sounds, weights and measures, balance, artifacts, distance imagery, abstract theories, and musical impressions. Every exhibit is buoyant and dynamic. Those loud noises that you hear erupting are screams of pure pleasure. The Brooklyn Children's Museum is delightful from the moment you arrive. The route is complicated, so call first if you're driving.

BROOKLYN HISTORICAL SOCIETY

OPEN:	Tues.-Sun. 2-5; Library open 10-4:45	**ENTRY:**	Adult $2.50
		TYPE:	Historical
CLOSED:	Sun. & Mon.	**ADDRESS:**	128 Pierrepont St.
SUB:	IRT #2,3,4 to Borough Hall	**TEL:**	718-624-0890
		GIFT SHOP:	No
BUS:	B25, B38, B41 to Borough Hall	**CAFE:**	No
		KIDS:	No
		RATING:	★★★

First of all, the museum building is one of Brooklyn's architectural treasures. Second, there are five major claims to fame in this borough: The Dodgers, Coney Island, the Brooklyn Bridge, the Navy Yard, and Brooklynites—all here in photos at the Schellens Gallery on the main floor.

Climb the broad staircase to the upstairs library, which is richly paneled in dark woods and the epitome of research libraries. Scholars fill the room, seeking data on early Brooklyn, scanning manuscripts, studying genealogy, or reading periodicals. The permanent exhibits downstairs range from a photographic portrayal of Brooklyn's Italian festivals to memorabilia of the Navy

Yard to the set from the kitchen of TV's "The Honeymooners."

Be certain to notice the photos in tribute to the Dodger fans who, 35 years later, remain undyingly faithful to their "Bums" despite their unforgivable departure to Los Angeles. Even if you aren't from Brooklyn, you've got to enjoy this visit.

BROOKLYN MUSEUM

OPEN:	*Wed.-Sun. 10-5*	TYPE:	*Fine Arts*
CLOSED:	*Mon., Tues. &*	ADDRESS:	*200 Eastern*
	Holidays		*Pkwy.*
SUB:	*IRT #2,3 to*	TEL:	*718-638-5000*
	Eastern Pkwy.	GIFT SHOP:	*Yes*
ENTRY:	*Adult $4; Sr. &*	CAFE:	*Yes*
	Student $2	KIDS:	*Yes*
		RATING:	★★★★

Five thousand years of culture await you at the Brooklyn Museum, which, believe it or not, opened its doors in 1877. Aside from having one of the most celebrated collections of Egyptian art in the country, the period rooms are spectacular as are the collections of American folk art and Oriental arts, the Print and Drawing Gallery, and the rotating exhibitions. Visit Rodin on the fifth floor, along with Sargent's watercolors, the Impressionist collection, the American paintings, and some gorgeous sculptures.

The museum is spacious and clean, and the art works are beautifully displayed. The museum shop is crammed full of art books, clothing, kitchenware, articles for the home, and so on. Allow some time for browsing. There's also a special children's gift shop—what a treat! Hear jazz on summer Sunday afternoons. This is one of New York's best museums.

NEW YORK AQUARIUM

OPEN:	*Daily 10-5;* *Holidays &* *summer* *weekends: 10-6*	TYPE:	*Zoological*
		ADDRESS:	*Surf Ave. at 8* *St., Brooklyn*
SUB:	*IND F,D to* *Coney Island*	TEL:	*718-265-3474*
		GIFT SHOP:	*Yes*
BUS:	*B36, B68 to* *Coney Island*	CAFE:	*Yes*
		KIDS:	*Yes*
ENTRY:	*Adult $4; Sr. &* *Student free*	RATING:	★★★

Aside from a few scattered hot dog stands and tourist shops along the boardwalk, this is one of the few attractions remaining in the once-legendary Coney Island. It's also the only aquarium of its kind in the New York area. The fish and marine life are from all of the world's oceans. The main attraction here is the underwater tank of beluga whales, but there are several sharks, dolphins, sea lions, a number of penguins, and some giant turtles. Did you know that the turtle has survived in the sea for millions of years?

All displays are clearly presented. A rare tropical fish collection is shown in one of the indoor tank buildings, along with hundreds of mysterious inhabitants of the sea. Aquatic events, shows, and feedings are continuous. All in all, it is an exciting spectacle.

The aquarium is well staffed and well maintained, and a fitting assortment of novelties is in the gift shop. And you can always stroll along Coney Island's three-and-a-half miles of beachfront for a remembrance of things past.

PROSPECT PARK ZOO

OPEN:	*Daily: Summer 11-5; Winter 11-4:30*	ADDRESS:	*Flatbush Ave. & Empire Blvd., Brooklyn*
SUB:	*IND D to Prospect Park*	TEL:	*718-965-6560*
		GIFT SHOP:	*Yes*
ENTRY:	*Free*	CAFE:	*Yes*
TYPE:	*Zoological*	KIDS:	*Yes*
		RATING:	★★★

As far as zoos are concerned, this one is quite small; in fact, it's the smallest of New York's zoos—Central Park, the Bronx Zoo, and Staten Island are the others—and draws family spectators out on leisurely weekends in Prospect Park. You'll see monkeys, bears, camels, zebras, elephants, and a seal pool right at the entrance. It's not the place out-of-towners frequent, although I can't imagine why anyone would prefer a more crowded place to see members of the animal kingdom. Besides, if you're in the neighborhood visiting the Botanical Gardens and Brooklyn Museum, why not drop in?

Be sure to telephone ahead. Restoration was begun in 1988 and may not be completed at this reading. The Lefferts Farmhouse next door, with a variety of farm animals, has been temporarily closed. When open, Lefferts can be visited summers only. Small is beautiful. This zoo certainly is both.

TRANSIT AUTHORITY MUSEUM

OPEN:	*Tues.-Fri. 10-4;* *Sat. 11-4*	**TYPE:**	*General*
CLOSED:	*Sun. & Mon.*	**ADDRESS:**	*Subway* *entrance at*
SUB:	*IRT 7th Ave.* *#2,3,4 to* *Borough Hall*		*Schermerhorn* *St. & Boerum* *Pl., Brooklyn*
BUS:	*B25, B41 to* *Borough Hall*	**TEL:**	*718-330-3060*
		GIFT SHOP:	*Yes*
ENTRY:	*Adult $2; Sr. &* *Student $1*	**CAFE:**	*No*
		KIDS:	*Yes*
		RATING:	★★★

You just won't believe, as you approach what looks like a subway entrance, that there is a museum inside, but there is! It's a former subway station and one of the most fun museums in Brooklyn. What nostalgia, with displays of early train models, turnstiles , signals, subway maps, fragments of subway tile art, fare collection devices, and tokens. There's a graffiti/photographic display that highlights New York's successful cleanup campaign.

Go downstairs for a station filled with assorted vintage subway trains just sitting there, but all shined up. Look for the wooden BMT car (c.1903), Coney Island trains, Bronx trains, and trains of all eras. Signs are clear, simple, and dated. Even if you've never ridden the subways of New York, this museum makes a great trip.

BRONX

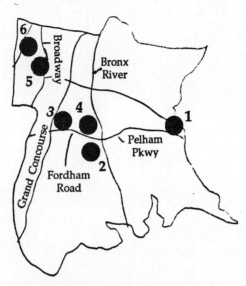

1. Bartow-Pell Mansion, p. 117
2. Bronx Zoo, p. 118
3. Edgar Allan Poe Cottage, p. 120
4. New York Botanical Garden, p. 121
5. Van Cortlandt Manor, p. 123
6. Wave Hill Center, p. 124

BARTOW-PELL MANSION

OPEN:	*Wed., Sat., Sun. 12-4*	ENTRY:	*Adult $2; Sr. & Student $1*
CLOSED:	*Thanksgiving, Christmas, New Year's Day, Easter*	TYPE:	*Historical*
		ADDRESS:	*Pelham Bay Pk.*
		TEL:	*212-885-1461*
		GIFT SHOP:	*No*
SUB:	*Lex #6 IRT to Pelham Park*	CAFE:	*No*
		KIDS:	*No*
		RATING:	★★★

This elegant and sophisticated mansion was passed down through generations of aristocratic and dignified Pells and Bartows, beginning in the 1650s. It portrays the upper-class rural lifestyle of the Bronx in the early 1800s. The original interior, starting with a magnificent spiral staircase, is of supreme stateliness. Each room is designed to perfection, mirroring the impeccable heritage of those two families.

Beautifully manicured lawns, terraces, and formal gardens top off the estate, and the lily pond is reminiscent of a Mediterranean villa. The stone Carriage House, a ten-minute walk from the main house, has a coach room, horse stalls, harness room, exhibition hall, and educational center. Its architecture alone is worth the walk. The entire setting is austere, with an intimate glimpse into the world of intimate people.

BRONX ZOO

OPEN:	*Daily year round: Mon.- Sat. 10-5; Sun. 10-5:30*	TYPE:	*Zoological*
		ADDRESS:	*Fordham Road at Bronx River Pkwy.*
SUB:	*IRT B'way. to Pelham Pkwy.*	TEL:	*212-367-1010*
		GIFT SHOP:	*Yes*
BUS:	*Liberty Exp. at Madison Ave. & 54 St.*	CAFE:	*Yes*
		KIDS:	*Yes*
ENTRY:	*Adult $2; Sr. & Student $1*	RATING:	★★★★

The zoo opened its gates around 1900. It would be imposssible to list all that is here because it's the largest zoological park in the country. Aside from the number of species represented, the condition of each animal is outstanding. If you entertain the notion of visiting every one of them, you'll need a two-week sojourn.

For starters, there's the World of Birds, the World of Darkness, a South American Wildlife exhibit, a Serpent House, an African Plain, a Rare Animals Range, and a

Children's Zoo, which is closed during winter months. The zoo's unrivaled *pièce de résistance* is a prized snow leopard collection.

Take either the tractor train, the Bengali Express, or the monorail for a spin. Or how about a camel? The zoo sponsors study programs and expeditions around the world. Bronx Zoo is open year round. It's a major tourist attraction and is definitely not for kids only. For an extra kick, try calling the zoo just to hear the "call of the wild" recorded greeting.

EDGAR ALLAN POE COTTAGE

OPEN:	*Wed.-Sat. 10-5; Sun. 1-5*	TYPE:	*Historical*
CLOSED:	*Mon., Tues. & Holidays*	ADDRESS:	*Kingsbridge Rd. & Grand Concourse*
SUB:	*IND D to Kingsbridge Rd.*	TEL:	*212-881-8900*
		GIFT SHOP:	*Yes*
BUS:	*Bx #1 to Kingsbridge Rd.*	CAFE:	*No*
		KIDS:	*No*
ENTRY:	*Donation*	RATING:	★★★

The museum is a tiny wooden cottage built in 1812, for which one year's rent was $100. Edgar Allan Poe, our illustrious poet, lived here for three years (1846-1849); his last years. During that time he penned some of his most magical works. "Annabelle Lee" is one of those masterpieces. We know that from early childhood to the moment of his death, Poe's life was tragic and painful, fraught with crises, illness, and melancholia.

There are, in the three simply furnished rooms of this frail cottage, memorabilia, photos, audio-visual presentations, and a guided tour for visitors. Shortly after his wife passed away, Poe died in 1849 at the age of 40, unhappy, alone, and unfulfilled. The small park named after Poe, with its bandshell gazebo, is a fitting front yard. Don't miss this penetrating look at a tragic poet.

NEW YORK BOTANICAL GARDEN

OPEN:	*Year round: Nov.-Mar. 10-6; Apr.-Oct. 8-7*	ENTRY:	*Suggested donation: Adult $1; Sr. & Student $.50*
CLOSED:	*Monday*	TYPE:	*Botanical Gardens*
SUB:	*IRT #4 to Pelham Pkwy.; IND D to Bedford Park*	ADDRESS:	*200 St. & Southern Blvd.*
BUS:	*Bx M11 to Pelham Pkwy.*	TEL:	*212-220-8700*
		GIFT SHOP:	*Yes*
		CAFE:	*Yes*
		KIDS:	*Yes*
		RATING:	★★★★

In 1890 the gardens, museum building, and conservatory were begun with help from Messrs. Vanderbilt, Morgan, and Carnegie. The carefully planted flora are mind-boggling, a green oasis amidst the concrete and steel canyons of the Bronx. Head first for the Haupt Conservatory, a 90-foot-high glass rotunda visible from afar, which has become the Garden's logo. It's a Victorian Crystal Palace of 11 distinctive glass pavilions.

There are a dozen different outdoor gardens, and the herbarium is a paradise for students of botany. Through the center of all this runs the Bronx River, complete with its original forest, huge rocks, waterfalls, and great trees, all here since the very beginning. Stop at the Terrace Cafe for a snack, then it's across the street to the Bronx Zoo. Bring your camera.

VAN CORTLANDT MANOR

OPEN:	*Tues.-Fri. 11-3; Sun. 1-5*	**TYPE:**	*Historical*
CLOSED:	*Sat., Mon. & Holidays*	**ADDRESS:**	*Van Cortlandt Park*
SUB:	*7th Ave. B'way. #1 to Van Cortland Park*	**TEL:**	*212-543-3344*
		GIFT SHOP:	*Yes*
		CAFE:	*No*
ENTRY:	*Adult $2; Sr. & Student $1*	**KIDS:**	*No*
		RATING:	*★★★*

Van Cortlandt Manor is one of a group of elegant colonial estates adopted by the Historic Hudson Valley Society. They've committed themselves to the preservation of America's heritage along the Hudson River from New York City to Albany. This area is called Croton-on-Hudson in the northernmost part of the Bronx.

The manor's original 1748 handmade structure of rough stone and brick is intact; its interior design is Dutch combined with Early American. The parlor, living room, kitchen, and dining room on the lower level are filled with period furnishings, and of the several bedrooms upstairs, one enjoys grand repute: George Washington really slept there. The entire home is simple and tasteful. Our compliments to the Society, which also holds year-round craft and art demonstrations, family activities, historic programs, and cooking classes.

WAVE HILL CENTER

OPEN:	*Mon.-Fri. 10-5:30; Sat., Sun. 10-4*	**ENTRY:**	*Adult $2; Sr. & Student $1*
CLOSED:	*Christmas, New Year's Day*	**TYPE:**	*Miscellaneous*
		ADDRESS:	*250 St. at Independence St.*
SUB:	*IRT 7th Ave. #1 to 231 St.; transfer to Bus #10 or #7*	**TEL:**	*212-549-3200*
		GIFT SHOP:	*Yes*
BUS:	*#1, 9 to 231 St.; transfer to Bus #10 or #7*	**CAFE:**	*No*
		KIDS:	*No*
		RATING:	*★★★*

This is more than an estate; it's an educational, scientific, and cultural institution high atop the Palisades at the northern tip of the Bronx in a district called Riverdale. There are actually two manor houses, which at one time or another hosted a number of charismatic tenants such as Teddy Roosevelt, Mark Twain, and Arturo Toscanini.

The mission of Wave Hill is to examine and demonstrate the dynamic relationships between natural processes and human institutions in such areas as science and art, archaeology, horticulture, and forest management. In short, it's a successful environmental center. The botanical gardens and the greenhouses are close to perfection. You're also free to wander the 28 acres for a truly astonishing Hudson River view, and if the time is right, treat yourself to a summer outdoor sculpture show. All this plus a concert hall. Wave Hill is one of New York's undiscovered sleepers.

STATEN ISLAND

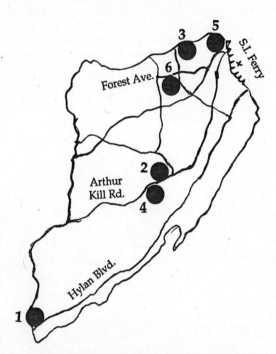

1. Conference House, p. 127
2. Jacques Marchais Center of Tibetan Art, p. 129
3. Snug Harbor Cultural Center, p. 131
4. Staten Island Historical Society/ Richmondtown Restoration, p. 132
5. Staten Island Institute of Arts and Sciences, p. 133
6. Staten Island Zoo, p. 135

CONFERENCE HOUSE

OPEN:	*Wed.-Sun. 1-4*	TYPE:	*Historical*
CLOSED:	*Mon. & Tues; months of Jan. & Feb.*	ADDRESS:	*7455 Hylan Blvd., Staten Island*
BUS:	*Staten Island Ferry, then #103 to Hylan Blvd.*	TEL:	*718-984-2086*
		GIFT SHOP:	*No*
		CAFE:	*No*
ENTRY:	*Adult $2; Sr. & Student $1*	KIDS:	*No*
		RATING:	★★★

On September 11, 1776, an important conference was held in this house. Benjamin Franklin, John Adams, and Edward Rutledge, all colonial rebels, were three of the American participants. The English side was represented by Admiral Lord Howe. The purpose of the conference was to attempt to stop the impending War of Independence. Despite that meeting, war was not averted.

This imposing stone house has been faithfully preserved, from its facade to its interior with gracious period furnishings. By the way, this is one of the few pre-Revolution houses in New York City still remaining. Be certain to go down to the basement kitchen. If you're not doing anything on some first Sunday of a month, there is an authentic 18th-century cooking and baking demonstration, and recipes are cheerfully shared.

JACQUES MARCHAIS CENTER OF TIBETAN ART

OPEN:	*May through Oct., Wed.-Sun. 1-5*	**ENTRY:**	*Adult $2.50; Sr. & Student $2*
CLOSED:	*Mon., Tues. & Holidays; and Nov. through Apr.*	**TYPE:**	*Fine Arts*
		ADDRESS:	*338 Lighthouse Ave., Staten Island*
BUS:	*Staten Island Ferry, then Bus #74 to Lighthouse Ave.*	**TEL:**	*718-987-3478*
		GIFT SHOP:	*Yes*
		CAFE:	*No*
		KIDS:	*No*
		RATING:	★★★

Jacques Marchais was really an assumed name of an American woman who nurtured both a passionate interest in Tibetan art and anonymity (her identity is still privileged information). It was her sea-going grandfather who first cultivated her curiosity for Asian art. He presented her with gifts from that region, which she accumulated until her marriage. Continuing on her own to enlarge her collection, she designed this Buddhist temple and filled it with the treasures you see.

The temple is small but quite beautiful and houses the largest private collection of Tibetan art in the Western World. The atmosphere is tranquil and serene; the temple brims with sensuous bronze images, paintings, silks, and samples of art from Tibet, China, Nepal, India, Japan, and Southeast Asia. Her library contains thousands of volumes on Oriental philosophy, art, and history. The lotus pond and terraced gardens are total nirvana. If you are a lover of Asian culture, this visit is a must.

SNUG HARBOR CULTURAL CENTER

OPEN:	*8-midnight, year round. Each section of this complex operates its own schedule*	ENTRY:	*Donation*
		TYPE:	*Miscellaneous*
		ADDRESS:	*914 Richmond Terrace, Staten Island*
		TEL:	*718-448-2500*
BUS:	*Staten Island Ferry, then #S4 bus to the Center*	GIFT SHOP:	*Yes*
		CAFE:	*Yes*
		KIDS:	*Yes*
		RATING:	★★★

In the early 1800s this sprawling 80-acre site was built as a haven for retired seamen, and in 1976 Staten Island acquired it for use as a Cultural Center. It includes botanical gardens, an art center, a day-care center, a fine arts school, a maritime center, restaurants, and a children's museum. Not all the buildings have been completely restored; however, those that have been are designed in a melange of architectural styles, to wit, Greek Revival, Beaux Arts, Gothic Revival, and Italian. Music and arts festivals and plays are constantly going on, and if you're an aspiring artist, it's possible to present a one-man (or woman) show by and for yourself. The modern and traditional sculptures scattered about are excellent. The complex is just a mile or so from the ferry. Why not spend the day?

STATEN ISLAND HISTORICAL SOCIETY/ RICHMONDTOWN RESTORATION

OPEN:	*Wed.- Sun. 1-5*	TYPE:	*Historical*
CLOSED:	*Mon. & Tues.*	ADDRESS:	*441 Clarke*
BUS:	*Staten Island*		*Ave., Staten*
	Ferry, then		*Island*
	#113 bus to	TEL:	*718-351-1617*
	Richmond Rd.	GIFT SHOP:	*Yes*
ENTRY:	*Adult $3; Sr. &*	CAFE:	*No*
	Student $1.50	KIDS:	*Yes*
		RATING:	*★★★*

In 1683 Staten Island was established as a county of New York. Two hundred years later it became known as Richmondtown. (Indeed, Staten Island is the borough of Richmond.) Half of the 25 buildings of the old village are open to the public. The entire mood is authentic and enjoyable. It's best to take one of the hour-and-a-half guided tours to visit the courthouse, elementary school, general store, and houses of the baker, basketmaker, butcher, and pottery maker. Drop by the grocery store for a bag of some of the best coffee around, and have it hand-ground to order by a gentleman who has just leaped out of a 300-year-old painting. Your receipt will be handwritten. The closest historic recreation you could compare this to might be Williamsburg, Virginia.

STATEN ISLAND INSTITUTE OF ARTS AND SCIENCES

OPEN:	*Mon.-Sat. 9-5; Sun. 1-5*	TYPE:	*Science*
BUS:	*Staten Island Ferry, then walk to Richmond Ter.*	ADDRESS:	*75 Stuvesant Pl., Staten Island*
ENTRY:	*Suggested donation: Adult $2; Sr. & Student $1*	TEL:	*718-727-1135*
		GIFT SHOP:	*Yes*
		CAFE:	*No*
		KIDS:	*Yes*
		RATING:	★★★

The Institute includes the Staten Island Museum, the Library and Archives, the Conservation Center, the Wildlife Refuge, the Park and Swamp. This is better than some museums, and it's extremely professional, housing all the arts, including decorative arts, fine arts, and techniques of printmaking. If you want to discover Staten Island's early history, here is the place for you to visit. And it's only three blocks from the ferry.

One of the desirable features of the art portion of this museum is its sensitivity to local artists, who are given as much space as the Old Masters. Because this is a rather small museum, the permanent exhibits have been scrupulously chosen to allow only the very best. The temporary exhibits are just as attentively offered. A film series pertaining to the arts is shown on Sundays, and only the very best are selected.

STATEN ISLAND ZOO

OPEN:	Daily 10-4:45; Wed. & Fri. 2-4:45	**ENTRY:**	Adult $2; Sr., Students & Children free
CLOSED:	Thanksgiving, Christmas, New Year's Day	**TYPE:** **ADDRESS:**	Zoological 614 Broadway, Staten Island
BUS:	Staten Island Ferry, then Bus #S48 to Broadway	**TEL:** **GIFT SHOP:** **CAFE:** **KIDS:** **RATING:**	718-442-3101 Yes Yes Yes ★★★

There's something about a zoo that brings families out together. Maybe it's the sharing of Mother Earth with all her creatures. At any rate, this one is a favorite of the Lower New York/Staten Island set. And did you know that this is New York City's biggest little zoo? Don't think that just because it's small, it doesn't have a fair variety of mammals, birds, fish, and small creatures.

This zoo also professes to own one of the largest and best collections of reptiles in the United States. The variety in their collection of rattlesnakes is impressive, and I'm not certain if I've seen an assemblage of (believe it or not) bats quite like this one. The Children's Center has some charming farm animals, and it's always a delight to visit with those gracefully pink flamingos.

KIDS' MUSEUMS

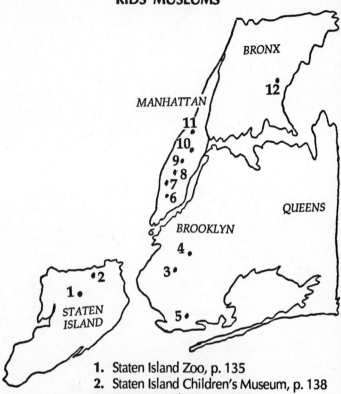

1. Staten Island Zoo, p. 135
2. Staten Island Children's Museum, p. 138
3. Prospect Park Zoo, p. 114
4. Brooklyn Children's Museum, p. 107
5. New York Aquarium, p. 112
6. Firefighting Museum, p. 13
7. Children's Museum of Manhattan, p. 137
8. The Marionette Theater, p. 138
9. American Museum of Natural History/
   Hayden Planetarium, pp. 72, 75
10. Metropolitan Museum of Art/Junior
    Museum, p. 62
11. Aunt Len's Doll and Toy Museum, p. 137
12. Bronx Zoo, p. 118

KIDS' MUSEUMS

Here are four museums designed mainly for kids. Adults are welcome, of course. Even though the four that are described here are lesser known, they are important enough to be mentioned. Also listed are museums that have their own sections in this book but hold special interest for children. Some give kids the opportunity to touch and feel exhibits, look through microscopes, and participate in scientific discoveries. Others simply afford visual pleasure and joy; and still others, each in its own unique way, provide a learning experience. Notice that they are spread out across New York's five boroughs.

The following four museums require a telephone call in advance:

AUNT LEN'S DOLL AND TOY MUSEUM
6 Hamilton Terrace (141 St.)
212-926-4172

Aunt Lèn, a retired school teacher, owns and operates this entertaining museum, with a collection of more than 15,000 dolls and teddy bears. Open only to order, so call first. $2 admission.

CHILDREN'S MUSEUM OF MANHATTAN
341 W. 54 St.
212-721-1234

Provides a setting for children to learn about art, science, and their world through participatory exhibits. Also offers a toddler program. This museum has recently had a fire and was forced to close for reparis. Date of reopening is unknown.

THE MARIONETTE THEATER
81 St. at Central Park West
212-988-9093
Open: Sat. only, performances at 12 and 3

Located in Central Park, the museum uses puppets and marionettes to create theater pieces with costumes, fancy sets, and music. Call ahead. Reservations required. $3 admission.

STATEN ISLAND CHILDREN'S MUSEUM
Snug Harbor Cultural Center (see main listing)
718-273-2060
Open: Wed.-Fri. 1-5; Sat., Sun. & Holidays 11-5
Closed: Mon. & Tues.

This is an innovative educational and cultural center where children learn through hands-on exhibits. $2 admission.

Kids will also enjoy a number of the "grown-up" attractions. Consult the alphabetical General Index for all of the following museums:

AMERICAN MUSEUM OF NATURAL HISTORY
BRONX ZOO
BROOKLYN CHILDREN'S MUSEUM
FIREFIGHTING MUSEUM
HAYDEN PLANETARIUM
METROPOLITAN MUSEUM OF ART/JUNIOR MUSEUM
NEW YORK AQUARIUM
PROSPECT PARK ZOO
STATEN ISLAND ZOO

INDEX BY TYPES OF MUSEUMS

MEDIA MUSEUMS

SCIENCE MUSEUMS

ZOOLOGICAL MUSEUMS

BOTANICAL GARDENS

ETHNIC MUSEUMS

HISTORICAL MUSEUMS

MUSEUMS KIDS WILL ENJOY

GENERAL INDEX